# CHALLENGES
# AND CHANGE

## AUSTRALIA'S INFORMATION SOCIETY

# CHALLENGES AND CHANGE

## AUSTRALIA'S INFORMATION SOCIETY

EDITED BY TREVOR BARR

Melbourne

Oxford University Press
in association with the
Commission for the Future

Oxford   Auckland   New York

OXFORD UNIVERSITY PRESS AUSTRALIA

Oxford   New York   Toronto   Delhi   Bombay
Calcutta   Madras   Karachi   Petaling Jaya
Singapore   Hong Kong   Tokyo   Nairobi
Dar es Salaam   Cape Town   Melbourne   Auckland
and associated companies in
Beirut Berlin Ibadan Nicosia

Oxford is a trade mark of Oxford University Press

National Library of Australia
Cataloguing-in-Publication data:

Challenges and change: Australia's information society.

Includes index.
ISBN 0 19 554855 8.

1. Information science — Social aspects — Australia.
2. Computers and civilization. 3. Information services
and state. I. Barr, Trevor, 1940-   .
II. Australia. Commission for the Future.

302.2'4'0994

Edited by Sarah Brenan
Designed by Steve Randles
Cover design by Linda Patullo
Typeset by Abb-typesetting Pty Ltd, Collingwood, Victoria
Printed by Impact Printing, Melbourne
Published by Oxford University Press,
253 Normanby Road, South Melbourne, Australia
on behalf of
the Australian Government Publishing Service
and the Commission for the Future

# CONTENTS

# PREFACE

This book of readings is published in association with the Commission
for the Future. The Commission was established by the Australian
government in 1985 to promote community awareness and understanding of developments in science and technology, and their potential impact on Australia in the future. Science and technology increasingly determine the sort of society we live in. The Commission's
fundamental purpose is to demonstrate that ordinary people need not
be the impotent victims of the march of science and technology; they
actually have choices, and can exercise them.

This publication emerged from discussions between Rhonda
Galbally, Director of the Commission for the Future, Louise Crossley,
also from the Commission, Clyde Garrow from CSIRO, Trevor Barr of
Swinburne Institute of Technology, and members of the Information
Policy and Assessments Branch of the Department of Science.

The essential purpose of this publication is to canvass major issues
about national information policy in Australia. Barry Jones has argued
that there needs to be wider recognition of a shift from a resource-
based to an information-based economy. For Don Lamberton, the
economy *is* an information system, yet many economists and politicians continue their discourse about economic policy merely in terms
of agriculture, mining and manufacturing. Ashley Goldsworthy shows
Australia's economic subservience to overseas interests in many fields
of information technology, and he chides the business sector in Australia for their failure to provide reasonable levels of support for
research and development. Thomas Mandeville sites Australia within
a new international economic order based on information products
and services.

A major dilemma for Australia's information society is that though
there are attractive prospects for economic growth based on information products and services, there are associated social problems.
High on the list of the agenda of social concerns for an information
society are issues such as personal autonomy and privacy, misuse of
information, and equity questions. Ian Reinecke points to the fears

that the social re-shaping of which computer and communications technologies are part will lead to divisions between information-rich and poor, and to a less just society. John Burke asks whether the advent of an information society will improve the prospects of individuals gaining access to information which they can translate into individually effective courses of action.

For Marie Keir, we are becoming a more self-service society. We can now readily help ourselves to all kinds of services by using the computer terminal. The clear lesson from her examples are that the effects of the growing use of computers in our society are often contradictory —both good and bad. Michael Kirby proposes ten information Commandments, and he stresses the importance of acting with resolution to defend elements of individual privacy where our future is likely to be increasingly shaped by the technology of information.

The book offers several applied offerings, in many senses. Averill Edwards shows how information technology has transformed virtually all aspects of library activities. Two papers address state government approaches to the development of information technology policy, that of Victoria and Western Australia.

A key role of the Commission for the Future is to raise technological questions and offer options about major decision-making for the future. Implicit in this collection of papers is the notion that an informative society is one with profound societal change for Australia.

# CHAPTER 1

# TOWARDS A NATIONAL INFORMATION POLICY*

## Barry Jones

In 1978, as a newly elected Federal backbencher, I asked myself (and anyone else who would listen) the following questions:

Is Australia passing through an economic revolution, marked by a reduced work-force in agriculture, manufacturing and some services, and the growth of an 'information society'? Is this a 'post-industrial' or a 'post-service' revolution? Is the concept worth examining? And if it is, what (if any) actions should we take? And when?

Similar questions were being posed overseas in the context of public policy, notably in the US, Japan, France and the UK, and by inter-governmental organizations, particularly the OECD. At the governmental level in Australia, interest was negligible; even to the extent of refusing to participate in relevant OECD studies.

In December 1981 an ALP task force report addressed the impact of new technology, including the information technologies, and pro-posed a 'national information policy'. The policy, the first by any major party in Australia, was adopted at the ALP National Conference in July 1982.

My book, *Sleepers, Wake!*, subtitled *Technology and the Future of Work*, was written and rewritten between December 1979 and October 1981 and published by Oxford University Press in March 1982. The book was a modest success in its first months, until a dramatic event on 26 October 1982 gave it best-seller status. This was a march on Par-liament House, Canberra, by unemployed steel and coal workers from Wollongong/Port Kembla which led to a scuffle and a door being broken down. Suddenly unemployment returned to the front pages. Some days later ABC's *Nationwide* did a three-part series on unem-ployment and technology featuring *Sleepers, Wake!*. The book then went through ten impressions in the next two years, has also been

---

* This chapter is the text of an address to a workshop on national information policy, held in Canberra on 3 December 1985.

translated into Japanese, Swedish and Chinese and will be the subject of a television mini-series. The book's title was taken from J. S. Bach's Cantata No.140, *Wachet auf!*—'Sleepers, wake! The watchman on the heights is calling . . .' With its publication, and the ALP's adoption of a national information policy, I began to feel more like the watchman on the heights, and less like a voice in the wilderness.

My central themes were these:

- Through the 1970s Australia and other technologically advanced societies had been passing through a 'post-industrial' revolution in which the nature of the production process had changed fundamentally. Manufacturing would decline as an employer for exactly the same reason that agriculture had declined over a century as the major employer: fewer people, using technology, could produce far more. I believed the 'post-industrial' revolution to be as significant for society as previous technological revolutions—the agricultural revolution of Neolithic times; the industrial revolution which began in the 1780s in Europe; and the electrical revolution of the 1800s in Europe and North America.
- Technology could change our perceptions of the world and increase individual capacity exponentially, but failure to come to grips with the social implications could lead to personal retardation rather than advancement.
- Concepts of work were likely (but not certain) to change, and the implications of future work/leisure/income trade-offs had to be examined.
- Technological change would have significant implications for education, communications and the political process; and the longer we dozed through these changes the more serious their implications would become.

Why did I, and do I, place so much emphasis on this concept of a 'post-industrial' or 'information' society?

Perhaps I should begin with a quotation: 'Sometime last year American business crossed a technological Rubicon. For the first time in our history, capital investment per office worker exceeded that per factory hand. Like it or not, information has finally surpassed material goods as our basic resource'. These are not the words of some academic (that derogatory term) sociologist, but appear in a paid article placed by AT&T in *High Technology* magazine. Just to show that this is not some ad-man's hype, the article goes on to quote Walter Wriston, ex-Citicorp chief, who likens information to a new form of capital, one that is arguably 'more critical to the future of the American economy than money capital'. Of course, forward-thinking 'academic' economists and sociologists have been saying the same thing for years. Newer is its widespread realization by the commercial sector, and even by governments.

By any accepted measure, Australia is an 'information society'. As a nation we must recognize, reluctantly or otherwise, the shift from a resource-based economy to an information-based one. The Treasurer, Paul Keating, has drawn attention to the need for Australia to develop 'brain-based' industries to supplement the 'resource-based' ones.

Of course, information has always been of central social and economic importance. But information technology is a transforming technology (much as electricity was): it changes everything it touches, it adds or subtracts economic value. Socially, access to information is increasingly the means to power, and exclusion implies a loss of capacity.

How prepared are we to meet the challenges of the 'information society'? What are the long-term effects on the economy, trade, scientific and technological capacity and employment? I have argued that Australia is already divided between the 'information-rich' and the 'information-poor': who is likely to benefit and who likely to be disadvantaged? If we are increasingly dependent on overseas information sources, what significance does this have for us as a nation?

The concept of a society in which brain-power replaces muscle-power, raw materials and energy as the major economic determinant still has a shocking novelty to many people who should know better. Tell people that more Australians are employed in the collection, processing and dissemination of information, broadly defined, than in farming, mining, manufacturing and construction combined, and they just won't believe it—even though the figures prove it.

I find a distinct resistance to new ideas in Canberra—or even a canvassing of new ones to stimulate debate. To many people set in authority, the shift from Keynes to Friedman represents enough intellectual excitement for one lifetime.

When three OECD Examiners visited Australia in August 1984 and April 1985 for their review of science policies, they noted a strongly anti-intellectual mood and commented that they heard pronouncements from a fixed position here that were commonplace in Europe and North America ten or fifteen years ago but have not been heard there since. They commented that ignorance and arrogance are a particularly dangerous combination.

We all acquire armour plating about our value systems.

The case of Galileo has now, after 369 years, been resolved in his favour by the Church. However, it is easy to understand the contemporary reaction to his heliocentric paradigm. Think of all those maps and atlases made obsolete! Think of the uncomfortable questions about God and man that Galileo's teaching raised. And who benefited by the new ideas? Who wanted them? And weren't they contrary to common sense and common observation? And might not a heliocentric universe arouse unrealistic budgetary expectations for telescopes and observatories? So I don't blame the Inquisition too much.

For my own part, I am glad not to have had to steer the Second Law of Thermodynamics through Cabinet. One can imagine the comments on the Cabinet submission. Strong objections would have been expressed about the broad sweep of the law: perhaps a reference to the IAC might have been suggested. Should it be left to the private sector to determine if the law had any validity: would not government intervention be seen as distorting the operation of market forces? If government administered the law, would it be on a full cost-recovery basis? Would it be preferable to adopt it but not publicize it? Would the implications of thermodynamics, too, create unrealistic budgetary expectations?

I approach information policy in the spirit of Pascal's celebrated wager. Assuming I am *right* and the implications of information policy are very serious, then if we take action we will benefit greatly and if we do not the detriment will also be great. If I am *wrong* and the implications are trivial (or even non-existent), then at the worst we will have wasted some time and resources on issues less important and engrossing than the deregulation of the tyre industry, self-government in the ACT and the future of dried fruits.

Let me reassure the faint-hearts. There is absolutely no risk that Australia will be among the first to embark on a serious examination of our information society. But I don't want us to be the last either.

We are trailing very far behind: consider this list of publications.

1971    D. M. Lamberton (ed.), *Economics, Information and Knowledge*, London

1972    Y. Masuda, *Social Impact of Computerization*, Tokyo

1973    OECD, *Information in 1985*, Paris

1977    M. U. Porat, *The Information Economy*, US Department of Commerce

1978    S. Nora & A. Minc, *L'informatisation de la Société: La Documentation Française*, Paris

1980    Y. Masuda, *The Information Society*, Tokyo

1982    *Planning Now for an Information Society: Tomorrow is too Late*, Science Council of Canada

1985    A. J. Cordell, *The Uneasy Eighties*, Science Council of Canada

I think that there is in Australia a strongly ingrained but erroneous cultural stereotype in which 'work' is equated with 'process work'. Old paradigms die hard! A generation ago, the shearer would have been identified as the typical Australian worker—although even then he would have been anachronistic. Many people overseas still see us essentially as rural workers. The stereotype that the typical Australian works on a production line in a factory is still very strongly held, despite labour force statistics to the contrary. When I talk to groups and ask people to identify a typical worker, in almost every case they will nominate a process worker in a factory, even though these now comprise less than one-sixth of the labour force. When I ask my audience to indicate how many members of their own families are process

workers, no hands go up. They invariably say: 'But my family is excep-
tional. Most people in *other* people's families are process workers'.

After speaking at a function with some mining industry executives, I
asked eight senior people at my table: 'Of the 2 060 000 new jobs
created in Australia in the period 1965–82, what percentage were in
manufacturing?'. The answers they offered were 30 per cent, 35 per
cent (four times), 40 per cent, 70 per cent and 80 per cent. The actual
figure is minus 7.3 per cent. They appeared as surprised by my figure
as I was astonished by theirs.

I think that these responses reflect the goods orientation of our economic thinking; that only tangibles have value, that services don't
create value, and that the only things worth producing are things that
hurt if you drop them on your foot! This leads to a defensive tendency
to segmentation and protecting the 'territorial imperative', so that
information = information technology = hardware = computers, and
communication = communication technology = hardware = telephone systems and satellites, with little if any concern about content,
social impact or context.

At the 1982 National Conference of the ALP—the one that adopted
the first national information policy—of 138 delegates and proxies,
only one was a blue-collar worker, and 133 were employed in 'information' occupations—MPs, lawyers, librarians, teachers, research
workers. By 1984, the last blue-collar worker had gone, and 143 of 148
delegates and proxies worked in 'information'.

Information *services* sold on established markets accounted for
about 34 per cent of Australia's GDP at factor cost in 1977–8. Information *goods* contributed a further 2 per cent of GDP. Marketed information services were a major growth sector, expanding one and a half
times over the period 1968 to 1977, and reflecting the growth of the
'information industries' as entities in their own right. And even these
figures are now more than nine years out of date! Our own eyes provide evidence of the mushrooming of this sector since 1978.

As an aside, it is difficult to derive measures of the 'information
economy' from national accounts statistics as currently collected and
presented. National (and international) accounts are still too much
concerned with what company people work for, rather than how they
actually spend their working hours; and what goods are made of,
rather than what they do, or what they are for.

A very useful study has recently been published by Tom Mandeville and Stuart Macdonald, of the University of Queensland, on the
information economy of Queensland. If I may quote from their conclusions:

The information sector has been growing, and growing rapidly, at a time when other
sectors of the Queensland economy have been stagnating. The information sector
has been creating jobs while other sectors have been reducing their employment.
The information sector has been both the source and the destination of much of the
new technology which is so radically altering the ways in which our economy and
society function. Finally, the information sector employs well over a third of all

employed Queenslanders: it is twice the size of the recognised manufacturing sector and almost four times the size of the primary sector. Not to take the information
sector seriously is indefensible.[1]

Not surprisingly, the survey shows that the industry that deals in
money (which after all is a purely symbolic form of information), the
finance/business services industry, has the highest proportion of
information workers, while agriculture has the lowest. Non-manu-
facturing firms reported about half of their workers as information
workers; manufacturing firms about a quarter.

I find the agriculture figure most interesting. Farmers obviously
require ready access to scientific and commercial information in order
to husband and market their crops and livestock—information (like
livestock prices) that they cannot generate 'in house' (or should I say,
'on farm') or information that is more conveniently generated by
specialists (such as data on agricultural chemicals). They are prepared
to obtain it on the open market and, as a result, agricultural information is in the vanguard of commercial videotex and other electronic
information services. Of course, agricultural extension and information services have always been well supported by governments in
Australia.

A study has also been completed on the Western Australian information economy. While less comprehensive than the Queensland
survey, the available statistics show that Western Australia has a large
and healthy information economy, even larger per capita than
Queensland. Interestingly, a large proportion of the new jobs created
in the 'information industries' in Western Australia over the period
1971 to 1984 went to women.

The significance of the 'information economy' has taken a long time
to begin penetrating parts of the national consciousness, and still has
not done so in the bureaucratic and political sectors, trades unions and
employers. Nor is it an issue to which the Australian print media have
devoted much space: to the press the information revolution means
news about the computer industry and supplements promoting
hardware. The human implications are largely ignored. This is uncon-
scionable. To take a parallel example, transport economics is not
simply car design. It takes into account the highway infrastructure,
road rules, road trauma, fuel policy, taxation, driver education, the
roles of public and private transport, environmental and social
impacts and more. Policy-makers and the media in Australia must
address the information economy in a similar manner, and this means
addressing the broad social and political implications of the information society too.

What potential does the increasing importance of information and
information technologies have for a re-configuration of political
power, for example? Is information to be vertically integrated, controlled from the top and used to shore up existing power structures? Or
can there be a horizontal model—with democratic access, strength-

ening the periphery relative to the centre, empowering the individual against the mass organization, the one against the many?

In their seminal report to the French government in 1978, Simon Nora and Alain Minc posed the challenges (or 'illusions') of information technology thus:

The pessimists emphasize the risks involved—rising unemployment, social rigidity, the vulgarization of life. They see computerization as a victory for the impersonal, repetitive nature of tasks and the elimination of jobs. It would solidify the unwieldiness and the hierarchical nature of organizations, reinforcing the omniscience of those 'in the know' while automatizing the others. All that would remain would be the computerizers and the computerized, the users and the used. The machine would no longer be a computer [*ordinateur*], a tool for calculating, remembering, and communicating, but a mysterious and anonymous order-giver [*ordonnateur*]. Society would become opaque, to itself and to its individual members, but at the same time dangerously transparent, to the detriment of freedom, to those possessed of the demiurgic technology and their masters.

On the other hand, the optimists believe that miracles are within reach, that computerization means information, information means culture, and culture means emancipation and democracy. Anything that increases access to information facilitates dialogue on a more flexible and personal level, encourages increased participation and more individual responsibilities, and strengthens the ability of the weak and the 'little man' to resist the encroachments of the Leviathan, the economic and social powers that be.

They conclude:

This dream and this nightmare at least share the same questions. Are we headed, regardless of appearances and alibis, toward a society that will use this new technology to reinforce the mechanisms of rigidity, authority, and domination? Or, on the other hand, will we know how to enhance adaptability, freedom, and communication in such a way that every citizen and every group can be responsible for itself?[2]

My own comment would be that neither scenario is inevitable. But we must assert our collective right to choose the best path for Australia.

I have stressed the extraordinary ambiguity of technology. What is the fundamental relationship between human capacity and technological capacity, between natural intelligence and artificial intelligence? If machines can do (or think) more, will humans need to do (and think) less?

In 1984, when the Labor government was re-elected, 8.6 per cent of adult Australians (up to 15 per cent in some electorates) found themselves baffled, not knowing what to do with three pieces of paper. How on earth are these failed voters able to make appropriate choices for themselves in an increasingly sophisticated technological world? Will the sheer complexity of modern science and technology—and the difficulty of providing adequate or appropriate information linkages with the community at large—lead to the development of a 'technocracy' and rule by an élite?

As Dame Leonie Kramer has commented, 'How can a democratic electorate be expected to make sophisticated political (or technological?)

judgements if its citizens cannot even understand the words used to frame the concepts?'. When the corpus of knowledge is doubling every few years, how can access to decision-making power (that is, information) be shared around? Is it impossible? Is it worth attempting?

One great hope in the computer age is that for the first time society will have the capacity to produce *individual* rather than mass responses to social problems, and that people will actually be able to choose options for themselves. Having said that, I express some anxiety that increasing technological dependence, combined with a lack of understanding of how the technology works and what it can do, may lead to a deterioration of confidence in personal competence.

The question of the wastage of human capacity does not rank high on our current political agenda, perhaps because little empirical data is available. I wonder how far Australians are the victims of the British model of 'education of minimal expectations': the concept—which we accept so readily—that hardly anybody (except the professional classes) is capable of doing anything well.

Within Australia, life chances in education and employment are essentially determined by postcodes. We assume without questioning that children from working-class areas either wouldn't want to extend and deepen their education, or couldn't do it even if they wanted to. But have we really done all we can to ensure that they have access to the information that they need, and the means to apply it? Should the public library system, for example, adopt a broader role? Should our schools be increasingly specialized, putting more emphasis on computers and science? Or is this the time for greater emphasis on general education, complementary to technology, aimed at promoting personal development (including literacy and the arts)? The question is absolutely fundamental and must be addressed now. It is a subject of enormous concern for parents. But I find little evidence that it is being addressed in the community at large.

These are all matters that are raised explicitly or implictly in the ALP's national information policy. The policy seeks to redress the enormous imbalances in information transfer and to ensure that the community grasps the significance of information itself as a factor of production and area for employment. It also addresses the attendant social and political implications of the 'information society'.

Taking the policy as my reference point, I have ranged over many economic, social and political issues in this chapter. Some might prefer to say rambled, genuinely believing that this diversity of concerns has little to unite it. I cannot agree. The common thread is information and information technologies and the consequences of Australia's transition to an information-intensive society, post-industrial society or information economy—call it what you will, the challenges remain the same. We cannot allow ourselves to remain blinkered by viewpoints or structures that have become outdated and irrelevant.

I have done my best over the past few years to raise national awareness about these issues, and I have asked the Commission for the
Future to give first priority to encouraging public debate on the implications, both benefits and threats, of an information society. I believe
passionately that there is now an urgent need to accept information as
a vital concept in government administration in Australia, and that
there are important actions that governments can and should take.

Until recently, government consideration of these issues has been
largely 'sectoral'. Some milestone reports, in particular those of the
Coombs Royal Commission on Australian government administration
and the Australian Law Reform Commission's 1983 report on privacy,
have taken a notably broader view of information policy questions. A
series of other inquiries and reports (among others the 1973 report of
the National Library's Scientific and Technological Information Services Enquiry Committee (STISEC), the 1976 Horton report on public
libraries and the 1979 report into industrial research and development
by the Senate Standing Committee on Science and the Environment)
are relevant to the development of information services and policy.
Regrettably, the recommendations of these inquiries were dealt with
piecemeal by the government of the day; or, more commonly, ignored
completely.

More recently, in response to a Caucus resolution to implement the
ALP national information policy, a series of interdepartmental meetings was convened under the chairmanship of my department. Responsible ministers agreed upon a framework for action that arose
from these meetings, which included public release of a discussion
paper on information policy issues and some form of wider consulta-
tion. The discussion paper 'A National Information Policy for Australia' was prepared by the Department of Science with the support of
a number of government departments and agencies. However, I must
emphasize that it is not a government policy document and has no
immediate budgetary implications. Its purpose is to raise community
awareness of information issues in the context of Commonwealth government policies and programmes, and to assist in moving towards a
national approach to information policy.

# PART I

# Information and the Economy

# CHAPTER 2

# THE AUSTRALIAN INFORMATION ECONOMY: A SECTORAL ANALYSIS

## Don Lamberton

Contemporary discussion of Australian economic policy does not even hint at the coming of the information age. Economists and politicians alike continue their discourse in terms of agriculture, mining and manufacturing, seemingly in ignorance of the facts that three out of four workers are not engaged in those sectors but are in the service sector and, more specifically, that 41.5 per cent of the labour force are accounted for by the information occupations, which produce, process or distribute information or operate the basic information infrastructure of the economy. The scientists and technologists, overly impressed by electronic gadgetry but each constrained by the boundaries of their own little part of the 'S and T' enterprise, continue to produce wild extrapolations of the benefits to society. By concentrating their attention on a component activity in the whole economy and asserting over-simplified causal relationships, these commentators are led to nonsensical statements about, for example, an 'R & D-led recovery'[1] or an estimate that 'Star Wars' technology will eventually yield private-sector sales of US$5 trillion to US$20 trillion.[2] All this makes it necessary to explain in some detail what is meant by the 'information economy', and makes available a number of entry points for the analysis to be attempted in this chapter.

Much of the present thinking is captured in a comment by Harlan Cleveland:

The information environment created by the explosive convergence of computers and modern telecommunications is full of example of Canutish behaviour. The trouble seems to be that we have carried over into our thinking about information concepts that used to work pretty well for the management of material things. But information (as enhanced by modern telecommunications and fast computers) is such a different kind of resource that our traditional ideas about 'control' and 'ownership' are somehow transmuted into folly.[3]

However, some really big questions are raised immediately. What precisely is meant by 'convergence' of these technologies? Has 'control' not always been central to management? (Jim Beniger's recently published The Control Revolution argues that control is the unifying element in a continuing process of change that goes back to the beginning of the industrial revolution.[4] From his perspective, the proliferation of micro-computers, satellite communications and artificial intelligence are further chapters in that revolution.) And whose vested interests lie behind the folly?

Revolutions are often slow processes. This is illustrated by the response of economic thought to the information revolution. Sixty-five years ago F. H. Knight wrote of 'the most thoroughgoing methods of dealing with uncertainty; i.e., by securing better knowledge of and control over the future'. Control of the future and increased power of prediction are, he added, 'closely interrelated, since the chief practical significance of knowledge is control, and both are closely identified with the general progress of civilization, the improvement of technology and the increase of knowledge'. 'Information' was 'one of the principal commodities' supplied by the economic organization. The information industry included market associations, trade journals, statistical bureaus, advertising, and a 'veritable swarming of experts and consultants in nearly every department of industrial life'. But unfortunately Knight dismissed these methods of dealing with uncertainty because they represented 'merely the objective of all rational conduct'.[5]

Thus Knight brushed aside the entire role of communication in the economy. In the information age, that role must be explored, beginning with definition.

A simple way of regarding human communication is to consider it as the sending from one person to another of meaningful messages. Such a minimal definition implies all the essential elements that we will have later to consider. Thus it presupposes a communicator and a receiver, and a relationship between them—a mutual awareness, or orientation of one to another. It implies an intention, especially on the part of the communicator; an external referent—what the message is about; a common language and some sharing of experience. Finally, it indicates some activity and change of state as a result of the act.[6]

Communication is part of the very fabric of society. It takes place at all levels between peoples and between institutions, from government to people, from people back to government, and through many channels both inter-personal and mediated.

The ways in which communication is used, the networks through which it flows, the structures of the media system, the regulatory framework for the system, and the decisions of the people who operate it, are all the outcome of communication *policies*. Policies are the principles, rules and guidelines on which the system is built and may be specifically formulated or remain largely implicit.

In any society, the communication system must fit organically into the political and socio-economic system of the State, and be consistent with its cultural values. While there are many common features in all communication systems, objectives, functions and policies will differ depending both on the degree of development of the country and its political philosophy.[7]

Even brief reflection raises contrasts and problems. 'Person' expands to peoples, institutions and governments. Today computers must perforce be added: a heading in the *Economist* once read, 'Computers gossip gaily to their foreign friends'.[8] The sending of 'meaningful messages' becomes communication or information flow. The intimate relationship between two people is lost in a communication *system*. These and other transformations pose difficult questions. How important is the speed and continuity of the information flow? What is the distribution of human information-processing capacities? What determines the changes in that distribution? To what extent can machines extend those capacities? Are there property rights, legal or otherwise established, in information? How important is so-called 'misinformation' and information redundancy? These complex and unsettled questions are addressed in both information science and information economics.

## THE LEGACY OF THE PAST

Kunz and Rittel summed up succinctly the problems of information science.

Today Information Science is confronted with three major handicaps: (a) to overcome its preoccupation with scientific and technical information, (b) to 'strip the eggshells' remaining from its ancestor disciplines, (c) to find its 'systems approach'. (a) is a consequence of the Weinberg Report where the sad state of the scientific and technical information system was depicted as a major bottleneck of national wellbeing. It has, however, become obvious that the whole gamut of information processes—and not only STI—is in a critical state, and that the non-STI processes pose even wickeder problems. (b) is due to the parenthood of librarianship and documentation science. Most of the emphasis of research and teaching is focussed on libraries and literature documentation, although there are so many other kinds of at least as important information systems. (c) is caused by the fascination with a 'systems approach' as it is supposed to have been useful in 'mission-oriented' projects of the military, of space endeavours, etc. Because information systems are also 'highly complex' and require 'multi- and inter-disciplinary' treatment this approach is believed to be the panacea. Unfortunately it does not work.[9]

The economy is an information system. In relation to the three major handicaps, this has distinct advantages. First, it extends the system from scientific and technical information to all types of market, technological and institutional information. Second, it helps 'strip the eggshells' by involving not only economists but also their fellow workers in a number of other disciplines (e.g., other social sciences, law, medicine, social work, engineering, and urban studies), as well as managers, politicians, and others who have need of economic analysis. Third, economics provides a ready-made and old 'systems approach', as the economist's effort to model the economic system goes back long before the modern fashion for systems analysis began.

The suggestion that the economy be viewed as an information system is not new. For example, Hayek saw the price system as a mechanism for communicating information.[10] Knowledge of relevant facts was dispersed among many people and prices served to co-ordinate the separate actions of different people. The interaction of people, each of whom possessed only partial knowledge, shaped events. In contrast to this process, which he believed ensured that detailed unorganized knowledge of particular circumstances of time or place would be promptly used, central planning faced an impossible informational problem. Of course, many did and still do disagree with his broad conclusion, being inclined to see advantages in centralization for some informational activities and in decentralization for others. A significant qualification to the Hayek thesis is that he was dealing with market information rather than scientific and technological information.

Those economists who might be described broadly as institutional economists have taken a wider view of the role of information. Accepting the idea that the economy is an information system, they have emphasized the control of information as a basis of monopoly and a source of inequality. Such an emphasis can be traced from Thorstein Veblen down to the present. For example, Starrett argues that 'the real advantage' in controlling the means of production 'does not necessarily depend on monopoly power (although such power may be an important factor), but can derive from having access to better information, or a better position in the institutional structure'.[11] A further point emphasized by the institutionalists is the difficulty of specifying precisely or modelling causal relationships once the role of information is acknowledged. 'In the process of economic activity, information is produced which conditions future behaviour and the production of future information, including values and preferences. Resource allocation, income and wealth distributions, and other facets of economic performance both influence and are influenced by the development of communication systems and methods'.[12]

Old-fashioned or neo–classical economists who took the institutional framework as given are rather perplexed by some of these recent developments. They are asked to accept institutional adjustment as a way of solving problems. They need to understand that institutional adjustment may have effects upon incentives, and informational effects. Major developments taking place in economics, viz., information economics, the economics of organization, transaction costs economics, and principal-agent theory, will be touched on later. First, a simple informational model of the economy is needed.

## AN INFORMATIONAL MODEL OF THE ECONOMY

Imagine a simple economy that produces only bread, furniture and cars. The structure of the economy and the different kinds of transactions are shown in Figure 1. Raw materials for bread, for example, are processed and pass from farm to flour mill to bakery through retailers until the bread is bought by households. These transactions are the solid arrows. There will also be transactions between pro-

**Figure 1   Transactions network in a hypothetical simple economy producing only bread, furniture and cars**

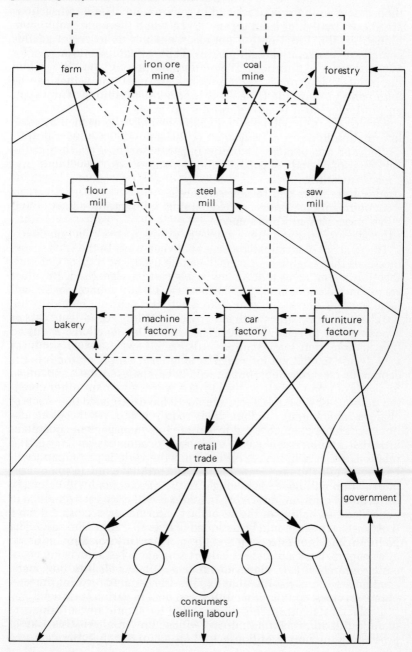

ducers: they all use cars and may need steel, timber and furniture. These transactions are the broken arrows. Finally, the households sell their labour to the producers and to government. These transactions are shown by lighter solid arrows. Even when there are many more industries, this input-output approach enables us to depict all this complexity in a relatively simple way. Table 1 enables us to answer for any industry the questions 'Where does output go?' and 'Where did the inputs come from?'. With a lot of hard work the values can be found and put into the table. This is only the beginning of an input-output table, but it is enough for our purposes.

Each transaction will be accompanied by and/or preceded by some information flows. A classification of these flows can be as follows:
- offers and acceptances, including in particular those concerning the transfer of custody of goods in transfer states, with or without payment in return;
- rules and orders and responses thereto;
- communications—messages containing information about activities, processes and preferences;
- threats, appeals, and other messages aiming to exert influence.[13]

The concept of terminal messages between units in the system, i.e., messages that establish a contract, can be used, and a matrix of message flows similar to that for materials can be visualized. But then some complications creep in. The message 'I'll buy your car for $x' will have been preceded by some search activity, possibly including the purchase of newspapers with advertisements for second-hand cars or a book guide to second-hand prices; the seller may have acquired information from television advertising. Likewise a steel producer may decide to contract for a regular long-term supply of iron ore. His economic research department will have analysed data and made forecasts of iron-ore prices, steel prices, wages and many other potential influences. His R & D department will have estimated the effects of changes in technology and ore-grade requirements. All these calculations will have been checked by calling in a management consultant firm that employs geologists, engineers, economists and industrial relations experts. In the course of all this the various participants will have used telephones, computers and the printed word. In some cases information will have been bought in the market (and will belong in the primary information sector); in others it will have been obtained in house (and so belong in the secondary information sector). All have their costs, which should be included in overall transaction costs. The point to be emphasized is that there is an information industry: newspapers, book publishers, advertising agencies, television, economic research, R & D, management consulting, geologists, engineers, economists, industrial relations experts, the people providing the telephone services, computer facilities, and data in various printed forms (e.g., official statistics). This suggests that we should revise Table 1 to include this information 'industry' or sector. An alternative way of presenting the notion of the sector is to point out that there are two

**Table 1    A simplified input-output table for the hypothetical economy**

| SELLERS \ BUYERS | 1 Farming | 2 Flour milling | 3 Baking | 4 Forestry | 5 Sawmilling | 6 Furniture manufacture | 7 Coal mining | 8 Iron-ore mining | 9 Steel mining | 10 Machine-tool manufacture | 11 Car manufacture | 12 Retail trading | 13 Household consumption | 14 Government | 15 Investment | 16 Exports | 17 Change in stocks | Total output |
|---|---|---|---|---|---|---|---|---|---|---|---|---|---|---|---|---|---|---|
| 1 Farming | ✓ | ✓ | | | | | | | | | | ✓ | ✓ | | | ✓ | ✓ | ✓ |
| 2 Flour milling | | | ✓ | | | | | | | | | ✓ | ✓ | | | ✓ | ✓ | ✓ |
| 3 Baking | | | | | | | | | | | | ✓ | ✓ | | | | | ✓ |
| 4 Forestry | | | | | ✓ | | ✓ | | | | | | | | | ✓ | | ✓ |
| 5 Sawmilling | ✓ | | | ✓ | ✓ | ✓ | ✓ | ✓ | ✓ | ✓ | ✓ | ✓ | ✓ | | | ✓ | | ✓ |
| 6 Furniture manufacture | | | | | | | | | | | | ✓ | ✓ | ✓ | ✓ | ✓ | ✓ | ✓ |
| 7 Coal mining | ✓ | ✓ | ✓ | | | | ✓ | ✓ | ✓ | ✓ | ✓ | ✓ | ✓ | | | | | ✓ |
| 8 Iron-ore mining | | | | | | | | | ✓ | | | | | | | ✓ | ✓ | ✓ |
| 9 Steel milling | | | | | | | | | | ✓ | ✓ | ✓ | | | | ✓ | ✓ | ✓ |
| 10 Machine-tool manufacture | | | | | | | | | | | | | | ✓ | ✓ | ✓ | ✓ | ✓ |
| 11 Car manufacture | | | | | | | | | | | | ✓ | ✓ | ✓ | ✓ | ✓ | ✓ | ✓ |
| 12 Retail trading | ✓ | | | | | | | | | | | | ✓ | ✓ | | | | ✓ |
| 13 Households selling labour | ✓ | ✓ | ✓ | ✓ | ✓ | ✓ | ✓ | ✓ | ✓ | ✓ | ✓ | ✓ | ✓ | ✓ | | | | |
| | | | | | | | | | | | | | ✓ | ✓ | ✓ | ✓ | ✓ | |

Gross national product

basic functions of the system: organizing and coping with change. The former is identified easily in the transaction costs mentioned earlier. The latter is clarified by considering the way economic modelling is normally carried out. Certain factors such as tastes, technology and government are recognized as important influences but are treated as exogenous—as operating from outside the model. The processes by which changes in those exogenous factors are brought about and implemented have not been spelt out. Those processes involve information stocks and flows and communication activities which require resource allocation. When these information activities are added to the information processes occasioned by the normal internal working of the economy, the aggregate represents the whole information sector.

## THE INFORMATION SECTOR

The importance of the information sector and its role within the economy can be demonstrated in several ways, for example, by analysing the occupations of people working in the economy. Table 2 shows the recent growth of the information labour force in Australia. Overall it

**Table 2    Information labour force as a percentage of economically active persons in Australia, 1971–81**

| COMPONENT | 1971 | 1981 |
|---|---|---|
| Information production | 5.2 | 6.4 |
|    Scientific and technical | 0.8 | 1.6 |
|    Consultative services | 2.4 | 3.0 |
|    Information gatherers | 0.3 | 0.2 |
| Information processors | 26.7 | 27.1 |
|    Administrative and managerial } Process control and supervisory } | 12.4 | 11.4 |
|    Clerical and related | 14.3 | 15.7 |
| Information distributors | 3.4 | 4.7 |
|    Educators | 2.9 | 4.0 |
|    Communication workers | 0.5 | 0.7 |
| Information infrastructure | 4.1 | 3.3 |
|    Information machine workers | 2.3 | 1.9 |
|    Postal and telecommunications | 1.8 | 1.4 |
| Total information | 39.4 | 41.5 |

Source: OECD, *Information Activities, Electronics and Telecommunications Technologies*, Paris, 1981 (plus 1984 updating of data base)

grew from 39.4 per cent of economically active persons in 1971 to 41.5 per cent in 1981. Two points merit attention. First, this growth is a continuation of a process that has been under way for many decades, at least since 1911.[14] Second, the most recent growth has been amongst the producers, processors and distributors, while the share of the labour force engaged in operating information machines and communication facilities has declined.

Earlier in this chapter a distinction was drawn between routine information activities and those causing change or responding to change. OECD statistics do not correspond exactly to this dichotomy. Nevertheless, they indicate that in Australia the numbers of people employed in routine information-handling occupations increased over the 1971–1981 decade from 22 per cent to only 23 per cent of the labour force. This is slower than the growth in scientific and technical information producers, consultative services, administrative and managerial information processors and educators. Overall the information occupations tended to be more resilient in adverse economic conditions, and those occupations made a significant contribution to growth in female participation rates.

A second way of viewing the information sector is in terms of the activities' contribution to gross domestic product. Table 3 provides

**Table 3   Changing contribution to GDP of Australia's primary information sector 1968–69 to 1977–78**

|  | % GDP | |
|---|---|---|
|  | 1968-69 | 1977-78 |
| **I  Information handling services** | | |
| 1  Knowledge production industries | | |
|    a)  Research, development and investigative | 0.33 | 0.60 |
|    b)  Private information services | 7.16 | 11.28 |
|       Legal | | |
|       Accounting, auditing, bookkeeping, etc. | | |
|       Architectural, engineering, technical | | |
|       Business services nec. | | |
|       Miscellaneous personal/repair | | |
| 2  Search, co-ordination and risk management industries | 5.46 | 8.04 |
|       Finance, insurance and real estate | | |
|       Miscellaneous | | |
| 3  Information distribution and communication industries | 10.12 | 14.25 |
|    a)  Education | | |
|       Libraries, museums and other community services | | |
|    b)  Media of communication | | |
|       Radio/TV broadcasting | | |
|       Newspapers and other printing/publishing | | |
|       Telegraph and telephone services | | |
|       Postal services | | |
|       Miscellaneous | | |
|                  Total | 23.07 | 34.17 |
| **II  Goods for information activities** | | |
| 1  Consumption and intermediate goods | 0.36 | 0.60 |
|       Office supplies, stationery and related items | | |
|       Photographic and optical goods, etc. | | |
|       Miscellaneous (radio, TV sets, watches, calculators, etc.) | | |
| 2  Investment goods | 1.36 | 1.34 |
|       Measuring and control instruments | | |
|       Office machinery | | |
|       Radio, TV and communications equipment | | |
|       Printing trades machinery and equipment | | |
|       Miscellaneous electronic components and accessories | | |
|                  Total | 1.72 | 1.94 |
| Total primary information sector (I & II) | 24.79 | 36.11 |

Source: OECD, *Information Activities*, op. cit.

this information in respect of the PRIS (primary information sector), i.e., those information goods and services that are traded, as distinct from the SIS (secondary information sector) which comprises equivalent goods and services provided in-house or internally that are not priced in a market.[15] The primary sector grew in a decade from 24.8 per cent of GDP to 36.1 per cent. Almost all this growth came in the information-handling services rather than in goods for information activities.

Table 4 effects a comparison of the primary and secondary sectors in terms of employment, in 1981. The PRIS as conventionally measured accounted for 20.2 per cent of people employed, and the SIS for a further 21.3 per cent. It should be noted, however, that some 240 000 workers in the PRIS are really non-information workers. This would reduce the PRIS to 16.3 per cent, so making the SIS significantly larger than the PRIS. These figures might be compared with those on the value-added basis; for 1977–78, the PRIS accounted for 16.2 per cent and SIS 15.4 per cent.[16]

There is no reason to expect a stable relationship between these two information sectors, nor for Australian experience to mirror that of other countries. There has been a tendency to see PRIS growth as a shift from in-house activity to purchased goods and services; a change viewed as desirable because it expands markets and might bring gains from specialization. However, this focuses on market activity and neglects the public sector. Furthermore, it neglects likely changes within the secondary sector. Trade in services, especially data services, can also have important effects on the PRIS/SIS balance. Finally, as the information sector includes infrastructure activity, trends there should be taken into account.

## INFORMATION ECONOMICS

A revision of economics that takes account of the role of information has won respectability over the last few years. The first general anthology appeared in 1971.[17] By 1985, information economics had been described as this generation's general framework for the formulation of any problem of economic efficiency[18] and as 'a fundamental and lasting contribution to economic analysis [that] has provided some of the micro–foundations for macro-economics . . . the basis for a New Theory of the Firm, of a New Welfare Economics, and of a Theory of Economic Organization (including a Comparison of Economic Systems . . .)'.[19] It is seen as 'a remarkable achievement in economic theory'[20] and 'information-based models' are said to have 'influenced macroeconomic thinking deeply'.[21]

It is difficult to summarize a development of such wide scope in a few paragraphs. The following are major points that can be made about information economics and its relevance to the Australian economy in the information age.

**Table 4  Numbers employed in the primary and secondary information sectors and in the non-information sector, Australia, 1981**

| Industry division | PRIMARY INFORMATION SECTOR | | | | SECONDARY INFORMATION SECTOR | | NON-INFORMATION SECTOR | | Total employed labour force |
|---|---|---|---|---|---|---|---|---|---|
| | Information workers | Non-information workers | Total | % of employed labour force | Total | % of employed labour force | Total | % of employed labour force | |
| A | – | – | – | – | 12 426 | 3.3 | 366.962 | 96.7 | 379 388 |
| B | 3 985 | 2 550 | 6 535 | 7.3 | 18 599 | 20.9 | 63 859 | 71.8 | 88 993 |
| C | 85 724 | 40 267 | 125 991 | 11.3 | 257 101 | 23.1 | 731 576 | 65.6 | 1 114 668 |
| D | – | – | – | – | 43 449 | 34.6 | 82 171 | 65.4 | 125 620 |
| E | – | – | – | – | 91 179 | 22.9 | 306 983 | 77.1 | 398 162 |
| F | 33 057 | 25 067 | 58 124 | 5.3 | 352 531 | 32.2 | 683 291 | 62.5 | 1 093 946 |
| G | – | – | – | – | 100 472 | 30.5 | 229 224 | 69.5 | 329 696 |
| H | 81 664 | 43 864 | 125 528 | 100.0 | – | – | – | – | 125 528 |
| I | 445 318 | 46 499 | 491 817 | 92.5 | 5 802 | 1.1 | 33 794 | 6.4 | 531 413 |
| J | – | – | – | – | 203 801 | 57.6 | 149 740 | 42.4 | 353 541 |
| K | 345 296 | 73 054 | 418 350 | 44.5 | 140 052 | 14.9 | 380 919 | 40.6 | 939 321 |
| L | 35 410 | 8 038 | 43 448 | 13.2 | 71 992 | 21.9 | 213 669 | 64.9 | 3 291 091 |
| M + N | – | – | – | – | 40 856 | 8.5 | 442 390 | 91.5 | 483 246 |
| Total | 1 030 454 | 239 337 | 1 269 791 | | 1 338 260 | | 1 684 580 | | 6 292 631 |

Source:  adapted from H.-J. Engelbrecht, 'An Exposition of the Information Sector Approach with Special Reference to Australia', *Prometheus* 3, 2 (1985), p. 379. The full table gives component figures for males and females.

Note:  Industry divisions are — A: Agriculture, forestry and fishery; B: Mining; C: Manufacturing; D: Electricity, gas and water; E: Construction; F: Wholesale and retail trade; G: Transport and storage; H: Communication; I: Finance, insurance, real estate and business services; J: Public administration and defence; K: Community services; L: Entertainment, recreation, hotels, restaurants and personal services; M & N: Non-classified/not stated.

- There is a great deal of difference between personal and group or organizational use of information. The division of information-gathering may well be the most fundamental form of the divison of labour.
- The cost of producing information is independent of the scale on which it is used.
- The greater part of the cost of information is often the cost incurred by the recipient.
- Learning takes time, so that there is a limit to the rate at which decision-makers can absorb information.
- There are usually significant information differentials within society in terms of possession of information, access to information and capacity to use information.
- The stock of information and the organizations created to handle information have the characteristics of capital.
- The output of the information sector is used significantly more by industry than consumers.
- The demand for information equipment, e.g., telecommunications equipment and computers, is a derived demand, dependent upon the demand for information transmitted and computations performed.
- The combination of uncertainty, indivisibility and the capital nature that characterizes information and information channels leaves the behaviour of organizations open to random influences; conversely, the successful pursuit of efficiency is likely to lead to a loss of responsiveness to change.
- The complexity of information activities makes information as a resource difficult to contain within the traditional mode of analysis based on production functions.
- The limitations on information as a commodity dictate a resort to organizations as an alternative to markets.
- Much time has been wasted in definitional debate. It is more fruitful to proceed as Arrow has done and say simply that 'information is a descriptive term for an economically interesting category of goods which has not hitherto been accorded much attention by economics theorists'.[22]

## THE AUSTRALIAN ECONOMY

Having set down some indicators of the importance of the information sector and its structural relationships with the rest of the Australian economy, some aspects of the performance of the economy can now be considered. Gruen[23] argues that the relatively poor growth performance is not new, most of the deterioration having occurred before 1973. Protection, restrictive trade practices, deteriorating terms of trade, real wage inflexibility, and public sector expansion are canvassed as causes. The first three are considered relevant before the

1970s, with real wage inflexibility having an important role since then. The public-sector expansion hypothesis is rejected. The paper probes briefly for more fundamental causes and turns to growth accounting and the now-familiar Olson thesis. These will be considered in turn.

## GROWTH ACCOUNTING

The application to Australia of a US analysis exploring why growth rates differed between countries[24] tended to yield the conclusion that technology and education had not achieved their full potential.[25] Surprisingly, Gruen does not mention the later work by Denison in which Denison confessed he did not know why the record suddenly turned so bad after 1973.[26] He argued that there was no unexplained retardation in the rate of productivity change until 1974 and that the drop in the rate at that time was abrupt and large. He provided the following catalogue of possible explanations:

A  Suggestions affecting advances in knowledge
   1  Curtailment of expenditures on R & D
   2  Decline in opportunity for major new advances
   3  Decline in Yankee ingenuity and deterioration of American technology
   4  Increased lag in the application of knowledge due to the aging of capital
B  Suggested effects of government regulations and taxation
   5  Diversion of input to comply with government regulation, except pollution and safety
   6  Government-imposed paperwork
   7  Regulation and taxation: diversion of executive attention
   8  Government regulation: delay of new projects
   9  Regulation and taxation: misallocation of resources
  10  Effects of high taxes on incentives and efficiency
  11  Capital gains provisions of the Revenue Act of 1969
C  Other suggestions affecting miscellaneous determinants
  12  'People don't want to work any more'
  13  Impairment of efficiency by inflation
  14  Lessening of competitive pressure and changes in the quality of management
  15  Rise in energy prices
  16  The 'shift to the services' and other structural changes
  17  Possible errors in the data.

Denison's catalogue points up the complexity of the process. In addition, it should be noted that, first, the retardation in the US was abrupt and large, so an explanation is needed for sudden rather than gradual change; second, the retardation was typical of the main industrial branches rather than concentrated in a few areas—communication was the only exception reported by Denison; third, international comparison might provide some clues—the *Economist*'s 'X factor' should have been evident elsewhere.[27]

A further question that might have been asked in the Australian context is whether the growth of the information sector had any bearing upon growth performance. The tendency to think of information as 'oil' that lubricates leads to an assessment that any increase is beneficial. This ignores the fact that 'expenditures on information are an investment'[28] and their productivity effects subject to considerations of capital structure. Complementarities have to be considered. What are the elements of information infrastructure and what is their optimal mix?[29] Certainly there has been substantial investment in information machines and services in the Australian economy and substantial growth in the information sector, but have the expected productivity gains been realized? In the US even the top players in the electronic information business are still waiting for the payoff. Some 1400 firms are squabbling over a US$1.6 billion market that had been predicted to reach US$16 billion by 1990.[30] As Strassman asks, when will the payoff come?[31] The need to consider this aspect of performance was first raised in 1982[32] and there has been supporting evidence of the difficulties experienced in both the private and public sectors.[33] There is, therefore, a need to explore further the interrelationships within the information sector and between that sector and the rest of the economy. This work is in progress at the Information Research Unit at the University of Queensland.

## THE OLSON THESIS

Gruen endorses the Olson thesis as an explanation of the performance of the Australian economy.[34] Briefly, Olson argues that individuals and firms are able, given stable conditions, to build networks that support their interests and impair dynamism and efficiency. Of course, there had been anticipations of this thesis in earlier literature, e.g., Schumpeter's 'petrified capitalism' and Kindleberger's 'aging economy'.[35] The point to be stressed here, however, is that the Olson thesis relates to government by interest-group pressure. As Norton points out, 'it addresses the political side of economic maturity. It refers only in passing to industry aging and not at all to the product cycle'.[36]

What is neglected by Olson and Gruen is the extension of the notion of organizational sclerosis to the firms themselves. Such reasoning (derived from the writings of K. J. Arrow) has already been presented as one of the key propositions in information economics. When the economic characteristics of information and information channels, i.e., organizations, are taken into account, further insight into the Olson networks is provided *and* the rigidities he stresses are seen to apply to the internal workings of firms—and governmental departments and agencies. This kind of sclerosis is economic rather than political.

This rival thesis has major implications for Australian policy. It suggests, for example, that policies that may successfully proceed 'along corporatist lines ... assembling our very narrowly based interest groups into more encompassing ones'[37] may nevertheless not reach the core of the problem—the organizational sclerosis suffered by Australian industry.

## HIGH TECHNOLOGY—A DARK SIDE

'[I]nformation technology and the communications industry are now major components of the Australian economy.'[38] Of course they overlap and are interconnected with the information sector. Such much so that some observers tend to equate information technology, high technology (or 'hitech' as it is sometimes called) and the information sector. Roach, for example, looks to the links between the information sector and firms that 'combine the flow of information with their skilled labor force and high technology to generate a knowledge-based "commodity" '—high technology including computers, office machines, communications equipment, instruments, industrial control and measuring devices, and miscellaneous electrical components and machinery.[39]

In the case of the US, 'it is increasingly important to view the extraordinary acceleration of spending on high technology as the complementary investment response to the rapid expansion of the information work force'.[40] This is supported by evidence of the structural relationships within the information sector and between that sector and the rest of the economy. The information-intensive industries buy the bulk of the high-technology goods, and high-technology investment and information-worker employment go together. If capital stock per worker in basic industrial activities is compared with that in the high-technology industries, there has been a dramatic convergence between these two components of the US overall capital/labour ratio, reaching relative parity in 1983.[41]

All this seems to be on the bright side and to favour increased investment to raise the capital investment available for use by Australian information workers, especially those involved in high-technology production. There is much spoken about this objective and a number of policy measures have been brought to bear on its attainment. There is, however, a dark side. As Roach points out, in the US the strong dollar and the widening trade deficit have taken a heavy toll on US high-technology producers. Between late 1982 and the third quarter of 1984, imports of high-technology equipment more than doubled, giving a 60 per cent increase in the market share of foreign-produced items.[42]

If the US effort to keep leadership in this area is leading to such a rise in imports, what are the Australian prospects? Australia's high-technology is still 'brought in, for the most part, from other countries, at high cost',[43] and analysis shows that information technology imports over the seven quarters to 31 March 1986 totalled more than car and oil imports, individually, and amounted to some 14 per cent of the nation's total import bill.[44] Achieving 'hitech' status may well continue to boost imports and accentuate balance of payments problems.

It might be argued that high-technology exports are the answer. However, 'getting such technology to market takes hard work and special resources, from research through to installation, from skilled human technicians and marketers, to advanced robotics, integrated manufacturing systems and practical, hard nosed business plans'.[45] Not surprisingly, Australia's export performance in high technology has been 'extremely poor in recent years ... Australia [is] spending something like $40 on high-technology imports for every $1 it [earns] on high-technology exports'.[46] Are the prospects likely to improve? In attempting to answer, it should be noted that great hopes have been held out for communications equipment, despite the fact that a US Office of Technology assessment finds Australia has a comparative advantage in invention in that activity of 49, compared with Japan's 142 and the Netherlands' 212—the index of 49 being the lowest for any of the seventeen industries in eleven countries studied![47]

## INFORMATION POLICY

Industrial policy is all too often equated with tariff policy in the Australian context.[48] The extent of the linkages between the information sector and all other economic activity should be a serious challenge to this view. Industrial policy must address information aspects of the economy. There are many reasons. First, industrial productivity is increasingly affected by information inputs. Second, trade in data services is increasing in importance and changing patterns of foreign investment. Third, the efficiency of management is shaped, according to the Arrow thesis, by information processes. Fourth, many policy measures are already directed to information provision as opposed to subsidies. Accordingly, industrial policy and information policy must be integrated. In the final analysis, both are directed to growth, efficiency and equity objectives.

## RESEARCH NEEDS

While research into the information economy and information processes within the economy has increased, and information policy was finally accepted as a topic to be discussed in a national seminar organized by the Federal Department of Science,[49] there has been scant support, public or private, for such investigation. Applications for funds are mostly refused and even inquiries about interest tend to meet with a 'We note ... ' or 'How very interesting ... ' response.

Perhaps the gravity of the research problem can best be illustrated by one simple contrast. The OECD figures for Australia cited in this chapter were belatedly provided by the Australian Bureau of Statistics. Almost all the information-sector work has been carried out at the

University of Queensland's Information Research Unit in collaboration with other researchers overseas.[50] In Japan, as early as 1982, the Ministry of Posts and Telecommunications carried out a survey on regional gaps in information flow for the promotion of regional settlement.[51] The quantity of information supply and information consumption was measured by prefecture. This measure of total information in all media included mail, telegrams, telephone, data communications, television broadcasting, radio broadcasting, newspapers, books and magazines, conversation, school education and theatre attendance. Australia can expect to wait a long time before such data collection is carried out—even though a research proposal was sketched as far back as 1973 by Arrow on receiving his Nobel Prize in economics.[52]

The very practical implication of all this is that Australia needs to think more about how to get new things onto the agenda of industry, commerce and government rather than dream about technological possibilities that may never eventuate. The prospects are conditioned by events within the information sector.

CHAPTER 3

# AN INTERNATIONAL COMPARISON

## Thomas Mandeville

Traditionally, economies have been thought to consist of agriculture, mining, manufacturing and service activities. However with the advent of the electronic computer in 1976 and the growing capacity since then of intelligent electronics to handle information, societies are becoming increasingly dominated by information. Global society would appear to be in transition from the industrial era, with its emphasis on factories, transport and the centralized mass society, to the information era with its emphasis on offices, computers, communications and the dispersed, diverse society. There are different ways of describing this phenomenon. One of the first pioneers to investigate it systematically was US economist Fritz Machlup. Back in 1962, he called it a 'knowledge economy'.[1] Later, in the early 1970s, Daniel Bell coined the term 'post-industrial'.[2] In recent years, following the work of Marc Porat,[3] the terms 'information economy' or 'information society' have come into vogue.

Information is becoming the prime resource. Its production, use and communication assumes the central importance in the information era that mass production of ordinary goods and services assumed in the industrial era. Industries that sell information services or produce information machines can be classified as information industries or activities. These services include education, telecommunications and postal services, electronic and print media, advertising, finance and insurance, consulting and libraries. Information goods industries include computer, communications and electronic equipment, scientific and measuring instruments, and office equipment. Taken together, such industries have been termed the primary information sector.

However industries comprising the primary information sector do not cover the only information activities in the economy. Non-information industries such as steel, motor vehicles, mining, transport, electricity and retailing also produce and consume information internally. Such information activities performed in house by organizations outside the primary information sector—essentially the office functions of industry and government—are termed the secondary information sector.

Drawing together all these primary and secondary elements delineates the aggregate information sector of the economy. In a nutshell this information sector consists of all office activities, the media, computers and telecommunications, education, and research and development.

Measuring the information sector precisely requires isolation from the traditional three sectors—agriculture and mining, manufacturing, and services—of those activities involving the production, processing, distribution, storage and consumption of information. A number of studies have categorized the labour force into information and non-information workers. Some people mainly produce information (e.g., scientific and technical workers and various consultative workers), others mainly process it (e.g., administration and managerial workers, clerical workers), while still others mainly distribute information (e.g., educators and media people). Taken together all these occupations define the aggregate information sector. An investigation of the growth of that sector over time in a number of countries clearly reveals long-term structural changes occurring world-wide.

## OVERSEAS TRENDS

According to Porat's study, the US was already an information economy in 1967. In that year, about 25 per cent of US GNP originated with information industries (the primary information sector), while the information requirements of planning, co-ordinating and managing the rest of the economy (the secondary information sector) accounted for an additional 21 per cent of US GNP. Thus the aggregate information sector involved about 46 per cent of the labour force, earning over 53 per cent of all labour income.

In Figure 2 the US labour force has been subdivided into four sectors —agriculture, industry, services and information—and relative movements are traced over the 1860–1980 period. In stage I, 1860–1906, the US was predominantly an agricultural society, with the largest group of the labour force being agricultural workers. In stage II, 1906–1954, industrial workers become the largest group, peaking at about 40 per cent of the labour force just after the Second World War. This period was the industrial phase of US society. From 1954 to 1980 (stage III), information workers become the largest group. Over the 1860–1980 period, the information sector grew from 5 per cent of the labour force to nearly 50 per cent. The information sector experienced its fastest rate of growth from the mid–1940s to the mid–1960s. This coincides with the invention, development and widespread application of computer technology.

The publication of Porat's study in 1977 prompted the Organization for Economic Cooperation and Development (OECD) to ask whether these changes had occurred only in the US or whether they represented a more general trend. Accordingly a statistical investigation of the information sector in member countries was carried out.[4] Nine countries participated in this exercise: Austria, Canada, Finland, France, Germany, Japan, Sweden, the UK and the US. Australia did not participate. The costs of this study in the late 1970s apparently proved prohibitive for a government uninterested in what was then reported as a radical view of the economy.[5]

**Figure 2    Four-sector aggregation of the US work force, 1860–1980 (using median estimates of information workers)**

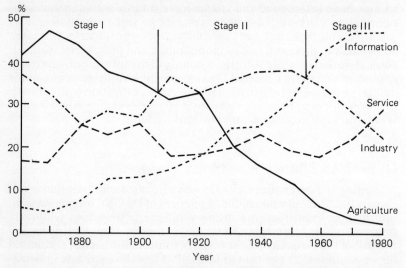

Source:    M. Porat, 'Global Implications of the Information Society', *Journal of Communication* 28, 1 (1978), p. 72

Results of the OECD study show that all participating countries have undergone profound structural changes with the growth of their information sectors since the 1950s (Figure 3). On average, the share of information workers in the labour force increased by about 3 per cent in each five-year period. The information sector now accounts for more than one-third of the labour force in these nine advanced countries.

It is only very recently that economists have begun to measure the information sector for less developed countries. Much of this work has been carried out by Neil Karunaratne and others as a result of co-operation between the Information Research Unit at the University of Queensland and the East–West Centre, University of Hawaii.[6] Most of these studies are still in progress or in the process of being published, and will not be reported on here.

**Figure 3  The growth of information occupations (as percentage of economically active persons)**

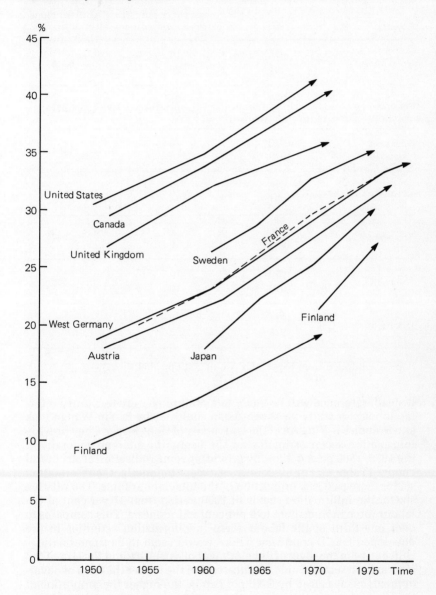

Source:   OECD, *Information Activities, Electronics and Telecommunications Techniques*, Paris, 1981, vol. 1, p. 25

**Table 4    The information sector in selected Asian Pacific countries**

| Country | Year | Percentage of labour force in information occupations | GNP per capita (US dollars) 1983 |
|---|---|---|---|
| Hong Kong | 1971 | 15 | 5316 |
| | 1981 | 23 | |
| Singapore | 1970 | 21 | 5219 |
| | 1980 | 27 | |
| Peninsular Malaysia | 1970 | 10 | 1961 |
| | 1979 | 15 | |
| Korea, Republic of | 1971 | 12 | 1884 |
| | 1981 | 14 | |
| Thailand | 1970 | 4 | 794 |
| | 1980 | 6 | |
| Philippines | 1970 | 10 | 656 |
| | 1978 | 10 | |
| Indonesia | 1971 | 6 | 510 |
| | 1978 | 5 | |

Source: compiled from Kwok and Au, op. cit., pp. 360, 362, 363

Instead, reference will be made to a preliminary cross-country information-sector study for seven Asian countries by R. Yin-Wang Kwok and Brenda Kit-Ying Au of the University of Hong Kong.[7] They provide information-sector estimates for the beginning and end generally of the 1970–1980 period, thereby providing some indication of structural change (Table 4). For all countries except Indonesia, the information sector increased as a proportion of the total labour force. The relative size of the information sector in 1980 varied from 27 per cent of the labour force in Singapore to 5 per cent in Indonesia. This compares to over one-third of the labour force in information activities in the developed OECD countries. There would seem to be some relationship between the level of development of a country and the size of the information sector. Table 4 indicates that the higher the level of development, as measured by GNP per capita, the higher the proportion of the labour force in the information sector (with the exception of Hong Kong).

While the domestic information sector of many countries has now been measured, not much work has gone into measuring information flows between nations. Internal structural changes associated with the emergence of the information economy within countries will naturally be increasingly reflected in the external economic activities and relationships of the individual economies. In short, the boundaries of the information sector extend beyond national borders.

Information-sector growth and technology-driven development in computers and telecommunications have in turn led to growth in the flow of international data communications—transborder data flows. Some industries, such as international banking and airlines, are now utterly dependent on transborder data flows.

Troublesome policy issues that have risen in tandem with the growth of transborder data flows include concern for privacy (see Chapter 13), the location of economic activity and employment, and issues of national sovereignty (see Chapter 12). Communication developments have dramatically changed the ways in which some multinational firms do business and where they locate various activities. These changes, in turn, have negative employment and trade implications for some countries and positive effects for others. The world has in some respects become a single region, and information flows freely where it will. However, the friction of distance still seems to hold. One OECD study shows that the bulk of international data traffic from a particular country is to its near neighbours.[8]

## THE AUSTRALIAN CONTEXT

An information economy would appear to be emerging in both the developed OECD countries and in the newly industrializing, less developed countries. How does Australia fit into these global trends? The first information-sector study in this country was conducted by Donald Lamberton of the University of Queensland in the 1970s, as part of the Telecom 2000 programme. This study similarly points to long-term economy-wide structural change towards increasing information intensity. The proportion of the Australian labour force classified as information workers was 8.5 per cent in 1911, 17.0 per cent in 1947, 25.5 per cent in 1966, and 27.5 per cent in 1971.[9] More recent OECD estimates put the Australian proportion of information workers at 39.4 per cent for 1979 and 41.5 per cent for 1981.[10] Australia is experiencing a transformation similar to that of the other OECD countries indicated in Figure 3.

One of the world's first regional information-sector studies has recently been carried out by the author and others at the University of Queensland for that State's economy.[11] The Queensland economy is commonly thought to be heavily concentrated in mining, agriculture, downstream manufacturing and some light industry. In the 1970s there was considerable State government emphasis on enticing major manufacturing projects to locate there. This involved huge complementary investments in infrastructure, such as the power station at

Gladstone and Tarong. Yet of the new jobs created in Queensland over the last decade, less than 5 per cent were generated in the agriculture, mining and manufacturing industries combined. The real boom in Queensland over the 1970–1981 period has been in the service and information industries. Queensland appears to be following national and international trends. The information sector in that State comprised about 36 per cent of the labour force in 1981.

Considering one facet of the international dimension of the information economy—transborder data flows—Australia does not seem to be experiencing this with the same intensity as many other developed countries. According to an OECD study, Australia is well below the OECD average in terms of relative numbers and growth rates of international data-carrying circuits, and in the proportion of international leased circuits carrying data traffic.[12] Recent case studies of large Australian firms confirm the above finding that, generally speaking—with important exceptions in banking and transport—Australian industry is not a keen user of international data communications, relying instead on the traditional telex and telephone media as its major means of international telecommunications.[13] Part of the reason is that whereas for most other OECD countries the bulk of international data traffic and trade is to neighbouring countries, Australia's major trading partners are not her near neighbours.

## POLICY IMPLICATIONS

The emergence of the information economy can be partly attributed to the development and widespread use of computers and other information technologies based on micro-electronics. But it may also be associated with the economic development process of nations. As Nerberger has observed: 'The larger the number of participants in the economic process, the greater the division of labour, the more complex the technological processes, the wider the assortment of goods and services an economic system produces, the more information intensive the economic process becomes'.[14]

As a resource, information has some odd characteristics. It can be used over and over again, its value is often enhanced by adding further information to it, and it is easily shared. The implications of these characteristics are only beginning to be understood.

There is need for both public and policy awareness of the importance of the information sector in Australia. With awareness, what new items should enter the agenda?

First, appropriate action to shift policy from almost total emphasis on the production of what is seen as 'real' wealth, that is, wealth in the form of tangible goods emanating from the tangible-goods sectors. Although most wealth no longer comes from these sectors, or in the form of tangible goods, economic policy still seems to assume that it does. Most wealth is now created in intangible form and most of that intangible wealth is information. Economic policies which fail to recognize this, which continue to assume that activities producing tangible wealth are the core of the economy on which all else is dependent, are likely to be irrelevant to the means by which most wealth may be produced and most employment created.

Second, the market system copes best when problems are well defined, information standardized, and when there is a low level of uncertainty. Where these conditions are not met, there is need for the invention of new forms of organizations—new ways of organizing social and economic activity.

Third, people—not capital, not energy, not natural resources not materials, but people—and the communication of information among them are the crucial inputs in today's economic activities. High-technology firms illustrate this point well. Perhaps our abundant natural resources distract our attention from this point. Japan's only resource is the Japanese, yet this Asian nation is probably the most successful one in the information era. Personal and organizational efficiency require a capacity to learn, ask questions and use information—in other words, the capacity to initiate change and adapt to it. General education can raise the quality of human capital as well as influence the speed with which skills change in response to demand. However, questions of general education should not be confused with the current computer worship. Because many information occupations are computer-related does not mean that everyone working in them must be a programmer. As more technology is built into such products, they require less skill to operate. A person does not have to be a mechanic to operate a car, a carpenter to operate a drill, or a technician to use a washing machine or video cassette recorder. Increasingly, people do not need to know programming languages to use computers or computer-related services.

Fourth, in Australia institutions, businesses, policy-makers, and the public need to develop more skill in scrapping what is outdated. In the economic sphere, exposure to international competition is a great help in this process. More basically, our concepts of work, the economy and society need updating.

Finally, perhaps a national information policy is needed to focus attention on these new realities. The Department of Science is moving in this direction.[15]

# CHAPTER 4

# EXPANDING ECONOMIC HORIZONS

## Ashley W. Goldsworthy

The information society predicted for decades has well and truly arrived. The collection, processing, storage, dissemination and management of information is the largest single industry in our economy, in terms of the percentage of the workforce employed. Analysis of the economy on a four-sector rather than the traditional three-sector basis shows in Australia that 'information-based' work already employs some 40 per cent of the workforce; more than agriculture, mining and manufacturing combined.[1]

Despite the unassailable evidence that the information society is here, there is an amazing reluctance within the Australian community to accept this fact. It is still treated by many in the community as an issue of, or for, the future. It is still regarded as tomorrow, and not today.

A prerequisite for the information society is information technology. The marriage of computer and communications technologies has given birth to a whole range of new technologies for the collection, processing, storage and transmission of information in all its forms. Computers and communications technologies are the *sine qua non* of the information society. It is the growth and proliferation of this technology which has opened up an almost endless multiplicity of uses in the handling of information.

Australia is in a very good position geographically, culturally, educationally and economically to assume a position of leadership in the information technology industry. We are ideally located within the Pacific basin as a developed, educated, English-speaking, wealthy nation. We have as our neighbours many less developed, less wealthy and less well-educated countries, with huge populations, tremendous economic potential, and they are developing very rapidly. We were, and still are, in a position to build on our advantages and take the initiative in developing indigenous information technology industries and become a supplier to neighbouring countries. We have failed abysmally to do that. We have let slip through our fingers opportunities that day by day are being hungrily grasped by other nations, who lack many of our advantages but who possess what we lack—the gumption and foresight to recognize the importance of information technology as the technology of the future.

We in Australia have been seduced by the 'lucky country' syndrome which has lulled us into a sense of false security. We have failed to appreciate the fundamental difference between our absolute standard of living, which is high, and our relative standard of living, which is slipping. One hundred years ago Australia's per capita income was the highest in the world—75 per cent higher than that of the United States. By 1920 Australia had dropped to fourth place, and by 1980 it had dropped to eleventh. Today I estimate we are probably fifteenth. If the current rate of decline continues, within a decade we will probably be behind Singapore, and within a generation behind South Korea. In 1953 Australia was the eighth largest exporter in the world; in 1973 it was twelfth; now we are twenty-third.[2] If over the past twenty years the Australian growth rate had been equal to the OECD average, the gross domestic product per capita would have been 10 per cent higher. That translates into $3000 for every household in Australia.

There have been many in recent years who have catalogued the dramatic decline in Australia's standing in economic terms compared with other developed nations. There has been plenty of evidence put before the community of the need to adopt new directions, to recognize the need for more concerted action. But these warnings have generally been ignored. Life is too comfortable to shake ourselves out of our cocoon of lethargy. Governments, at all levels, in the past decade and more have failed miserably to address the issue of information technology in Australia. The mañana philosophy permeates all levels of our society. At the highest levels there always seems to be a more immediate, a more pressing problem which has to be solved. High technology, and specifically information technology, is not seen to be urgent or important.

The tremendous growth in information handling and transmission will pose enormous problems in relation to the changing nature of work, changes in the structure of the workforce, privacy, continuing education, leisure activities, and perhaps some of the fundamental values of our society. The all-pervasive nature of the changes in society brought about by the spread of information technologies constitutes a revolution rather than simply a series of innovations. It is a revolution because of the radical nature of the change being brought about; it is a revolution because of the tremendous rate of change that is taking place; it is a revolution because it impinges on every facet of our lifestyle; it is a revolution because life will never be the same again.

A phrase has been coined which I believe encapsulates the importance of information technology for the future: 'Semi-conductors are the crude oil of the 1980s'. By the turn of the century information will rank in importance alongside energy as an economic commodity.

## TECHNOLOGICAL COLONIZATION

In 1988 Australia will be celebrating the bicentenary of its founding. Our history started as a colony and it took a very long time before we shook ourselves free from the fact and image of colonization and stood upon our own feet as an independent nation. It is somewhat sobering, therefore, to realize that Australia at the moment faces a very real danger of entering another period of utmost dependency on other nations. Australia is becoming almost totally dependent on other countries for its high technology. Moreover, apart from over-dependency, we are losing enormous opportunities to increase export earnings and employment opportunities in this country, at a time when both are vitally important. Our overseas balance of trade is perennially in a precarious situation because of Australia's heavy dependence on world prices for its primary and mineral products. In periods such as 1985–86, when world commodity prices hit rock bottom, Australia's export earnings and balance of trade deficit were most unsatisfactory. In these circumstances it is vital for Australia to develop replacement industries and markets which will reduce our over-dependency on our historical export products.

At the moment, Australia is completely dependent upon overseas supplies for almost all its computer-based requirements. This reliance extends from the purchase of new equipment through to the supply of spare parts. Without access to computer systems from the United States, Japan and the United Kingdom, Australia would face an impossible situation. We have failed to develop our own indigenous high-technology industries. We constantly see arguments put forward that Australia does not need this sort of capacity; we are too small a nation to be able to effectively develop such a capacity; and the resources, financial and otherwise, needed to effectively do this do not exist within Australia. These arguments ignore what other countries, even smaller than Australia, have achieved in developing high-technology industries. It is somewhat sobering to look at the latest figures available on the performance of Australia and some of its OECD partners in this respect.

An examination of Table 5, showing trade in selected technology-based products, highlights an abysmal situation as far as Australia is concerned. Table 5 shows that Australia's exports of technology-based products per capita are exceeded by every OECD nation except Greece, Iceland and Turkey; in other words we rank twenty-first out of the twenty-four OECD nations. This is an appalling indictment of our failure to recognize the importance of high value-added industries and to develop them. The usual arguments of small population are destroyed by the performances of countries such as Belgium, Sweden, Ireland, Denmark, Austria, Norway, Finland and New Zealand. There really is no satisfactory excuse for our continued failure to address this crucial aspect of our economy. Switzerland exports 33 times as much per capita as Australia. If Australia exported technology-based products at the same level as Switzerland, our exports would, in 1983,

**Table 5    Trade in selected technology-based products OECD nations, 1983**

| Country | Population (million persons) | Exports (US$m) | Imports (US$m) | Ratio of exports to imports | Per capita exports (US$ per person) |
|---|---|---|---|---|---|
| Switzerland | 6.5 | 15 785 | 8 634 | 1.83 | 2 426.5 |
| Netherlands | 14.4 | 18 861 | 15 235 | 1.24 | 1 313.3 |
| Belgium | 9.9 | 11 428 | 11 402 | 1.00 | 1 159.0 |
| Federal Republic of Germany | 61.4 | 69 592 | 35 726 | 1.95 | 1 133.0 |
| Sweden | 8.3 | 8 832 | 8 642 | 1.02 | 1 060.2 |
| Ireland | 3.5 | 3 461 | 2 854 | 1.21 | 986.1 |
| Denmark | 5.1 | 4 356 | 4 404 | 0.99 | 851.7 |
| Austria | 7.5 | 5 513 | 6 018 | 0.92 | 730.3 |
| Japan | 119.3 | 68 096 | 14 737 | 4.62 | 571.0 |
| UK | 56.4 | 32 067 | 30 371 | 1.06 | 568.9 |
| France | 54.4 | 30 005 | 28 385 | 1.06 | 551.2 |
| Norway | 4.1 | 2 012 | 3 885 | 0.52 | 487.2 |
| Finland | 4.4 | 2 364 | 3 992 | 0.59 | 486.2 |
| Canada | 24.9 | 11 177 | 21 030 | 0.53 | 448.8 |
| Italy | 56.9 | 20 682 | 17 534 | 1.18 | 363.9 |
| USA | 234.5 | 97 983 | 63 762 | 1.25 | 340.2 |
| Yugoslavia | 22.9 | 3 047 | 3 574 | 0.85 | 133.3 |
| New Zealand | 3.2 | 354 | 1 937 | 0.18 | 110.5 |
| Spain | 38.2 | 3 551 | 7 154 | 0.50 | 92.9 |
| Portugal | 10.0 | 872 | 2 326 | 0.38 | 86.4 |
| Australia | 15.4 | 1 120 | 7 343 | 0.15 | 72.8 |
| Greece | 9.9 | 288 | 2 101 | 0.14 | 29.2 |
| Iceland | 0.2 | 2.8 | 201 | 0.01 | 11.6 |
| Turkey | 47.8 | 419 | 3 509 | 0.12 | 8.8 |

Source:   Department of Science, Science and Technology Statement, November, 1985, p. 52

have totalled US$37 billion, as compared with the US$1.1 billion that we actually did export. The figures speak for themselves. Think of what that increase in technology-based exports would do to Australia's balance of trade deficit. It would completely change our economic situation and the nature of our domestic economy.

When we are considering expanding economic horizons it is difficult, in fact impossible, to go beyond the critical importance of developing import-substitution industries in high value-added, technology-based products and services. Information technology is a vital component of many of these industries. Information technology equipment itself is a significant part of our imports.

Another factor highlighted by Table 5 is Australia's high spending on imports of technology-based products compared with what we earn on exports. We spend $1 on imports for every 15c we earn on exports. This underlines our heavy dependence on the importation of high technology and reinforces the position of Australia as a technological colony. It is little comfort to know that Australia's performance was better some years ago. In 1978, for example, our exports per capita were some $170 and at that time our export/import ratio was about 0.28. We have fairly steadily declined since then.

It must be patently obvious that expanding economic horizons are inevitably tied to high-technology, knowledge-based industries. Knowledge-based industries are the industries of the future, and the prerequisite technology is information technology. The vital ingredient for developing such industries is human intellectual skills, and the importance of this factor is discussed below. Future industrial strategy and future economic planning must recognize the importance of high value-added, technology-based and knowledge-intensive industries. Information technologies have all these characteristics, yet Australia so far has shown a pitiful lack of awareness of what we should be doing to plan for and benefit from these developments. Table 6 highlights our unsatisfactory situation. The table shows the value of imports and exports of computer equipment for Australia and five other countries in 1981. The countries chosen for comparison include some that are larger and some that are smaller than Australia in population. The figures speak for themselves.

**Table 6    Imports and exports of computer equipment by selected countries, 1981**

| | US$ million | | |
| | Imports | Exports | Ratio of imports to exports |
| --- | --- | --- | --- |
| UK | 1 756 | 1 422 | 1.23 |
| Japan | 732 | 542 | 1.35 |
| Sweden | 364 | 488 | 0.87 |
| Spain | 325 | 114 | 2.84 |
| Ireland | 122 | 350 | 0.35 |
| Australia | 377 | 9 | 41.04 |

Source: *Australian Director*, February 1983, p. 31

Table 7, showing imports into and exports out of Australia of information technology products, shows the same depressing picture. It highlights our abysmally poor performance in the ratio of imports to exports. The ratio has become progressively worse each year since 1982–83. How much longer are we going to let this trend continue before we realize that it is a pattern of disaster for the future? The

**Table 7    Australia's information technology imports and exports**

|  | 1982-83 | 1983-84 | 1984-85 |
|---|---|---|---|
| Imports | 1 627 | 2 108 | 2 834 |
| Exports | 161 | 169 | 222 |
| Ratio | 10:1 | 12:1 | 13:1 |

Note: imports and exports comprise Australian import commodity classifications 75 and 76—office machines, automatic data processing equipment, telecommunications and sound recording and reproducing apparatus and equipment

absolute values of exports are also disgraceful when compared with other countries, as discussed above.

It might be useful perhaps to give one or two specific examples of potential industry niches in the information technology sector that could be effectively developed in Australia. There are already hundreds of Australian companies in the business of producing computer hardware, computer software, and a variety of communications equipment. Some of these have been very successful, not only in Australia, but in overseas markets as well. There are undoubtedly some market niches which can be filled by innovative and aggressive entrepreneurs in Australia, or any other country for that matter. Similarly, there are areas of information technology in which it would be foolish for us to compete, for example, large-scale mainframe computer manufacturing operations.

Not enough attention has been paid to identifying specific market needs that provide sufficient demand to support a supplier. Having identified such market opportunities we must be prepared to give greater support to developing the necessary infrastructures to help the potential suppliers. As an example, a report in October 1985 by the Department of Industry, Technology and Commerce into opportunities in the fields of optical communications and fibre optics demonstrated a substantial potential.[3] The optical communications and fibre optics market is expanding rapidly world-wide. The fibre optics market in particular is experiencing a growth rate of between 40 and 60 per cent per year, reflecting the high-growth nature of the telecommunications industry. The report reveals an impressive amount of high-quality research being carried out in Australia in this field. However, one of the more disappointing aspects is that only about one-tenth of R & D projects have so far led to penetration of the commercial, domestic or export market. This is typical of much of Australian experience in failing to bring to commercial fruition the results of research activities. However, the report does identify considerable manufacturing and industrial activity in Australia, including penetration of some export markets, such as the USA for optical fibre cable, optical terminal and link equipment; New Zealand for optical fibre cable and complete systems; and South-East Asia for fibres.

The report estimates that a total Australian market of $60 million would exist by 1990 and $300 million by 1995. This is an enormous potential and it is imperative that it be satisfied, as far as possible, by Australian firms and not overseas suppliers. If this is to be achieved there will need to be concerted effort, both by government and industry, to ensure that infrastructure needs are met. For example, adequate skilled labour is an essential prerequisite and there must be an increased industry awareness of the technology and its applications. A policy of government purchase is also an essential ingredient for success, as in most high-technology industries.

Apart from the Australian domestic market, the potential for developing large exports is very significant. The world market for optical communication components and systems is expected to reach $15 billion by 1995. In a submission to the investigating team, the Institution of Radio and Electronics Engineers Australia pointed out that France predicts a growth in her fibre-optic market from 400 million French francs in 1984 to almost 800 million in 1990; Japan predicts that her fibre-optic communication system production will increase 35 per cent annually between 1980 and 2000, reaching $1.5 billion by 1990 and $18 billion by the year 2000; for the US, it is predicted that the market for long-haul fibre-optic systems will increase from $400 million in 1984 to $1.5 billion by 1988. The sheer size of these markets opens up enormous opportunities for quality products.

Another useful example of a market segment that could be of relevance to Australia is in computer systems design, especially of knowledge-based or expert systems. This is an important area of software development. A working paper by the Department of Industry, Technology and Commerce, issued in February 1986, looked at Australian capabilities and opportunities in the field of expert systems, and the overall assessment was depressing.[4] The report points out that even if Australia were to hold a single percentage share of the total world market, this would amount to somewhere between US$15 and US$25 million per annum by 1995. It suggests that Australians should be aiming for at least 10 per cent of the world market— a market of US$250 million in 1995. It is suggested that this is a conservative estimate, and other forecasts are much more optimistic than this. Obviously the potential is there. The question is, can Australia meet the challenge?

Australia does have an acknowledged expertise in this area but we face the usual problem (in Australia) of failing to convert our R & D into commercial products. The report identifies several reasons for this: fragmentation within and between sectors; negligible expenditure; lack of national co-ordination; 'brain drain'; inadequate training mechanisms; and inadequate marketing mechanisms. These difficulties could, and do, apply to many other sectors in information technology, and underline the difficulty Australian firms face in competing with overseas suppliers.

A particular problem in the field of expert systems is that much of

Australia's expertise is concentrated in the academic sector, and it is particularly difficult to convert research into commercial products in this sector. Overseas in recent years we have seen a national approach to areas such as this. For example, in the UK we have the Alvey programme; in Japan the Institute for New Generation Computer Technology's ten-year plan; the US Strategic Computing Initiatives in the defence area; and in Europe the ESPRIT and EUREKA plans. Such a national programme for Australia could be a useful way to move in the field of expert systems.

We see, therefore, a field which is very poorly developed in Australia, but one which holds enormous potential economic advantages if we can get our act together.

One consequence of expanding economic opportunities should be increased employment opportunities. In this respect, high-technology industries such as information technology are particularly important. Research in the United States has clearly shown that high-technology industries generate, in proportion to investment, far more new jobs than traditional or established industries. In the high-technology firms, in areas such as computers and micro-electronics, each million dollars of turnover creates some forty times as many new jobs as the same investment in traditional industries such as car manufacturing and steel making. These employment-generating characteristics increase the desirability of concentrating on information technology industries as a vital sector of Australia's future economic development. There is little doubt that by the end of this century the information technology industry will be the largest single industry in the world. Similarly, ancillary industries within the information technology field will also grow very rapidly. This means that in the years to come information technologies will play a dominant role in the economic situation.

Importing technology means exporting jobs. We must take positive steps immediately to create, develop and support high-technology industries. Australians have been accused of suffering from a 'technological cringe'. This all-too-pervasive apathy must be excised, otherwise we shall continue to regard anything made overseas as inevitably better than what we can do ourselves. This is not true and the sooner we accept the fact that we can compete, and compete on equal terms, the sooner we will address, and redress, the unenviable situation we find ourselves in. It is perhaps sobering to realize that one company in Finland exports more computer-based technology than Australia does as a nation.

The threat of technological colonization is a very real one. It is rapidly looming as one of the most serious issues facing this country.

## RESEARCH AND DEVELOPMENT

One cannot discuss the economic opportunities created by information technology without at the same time recognizing that a dynamic and flexible local R & D effort is one of the essential prerequisites for an effective indigenous capability. Without this not only will we lack the essential reservoir of knowledge and skills in basic research, but we will lack the capability to translate the results of research into viable commercial products. This is one of the major problems we face. Australia, with 0.3 per cent of the world's population, produces 2 per cent of research, 0.7 per cent of patents, but only 0.1 per cent of final products or sales.

Table 8 shows comparative R & D activity in OECD nations. The countries are grouped into three categories based on the percentage of gross domestic product (GDP) spent on domestic research and development. Australia falls within the middle group of medium R & D performers.

**Table 8    R & D effort in OECD countries compared***

| Country | R & D employment as % of total workforce | Gross expenditure on R & D as % of GDP | R & D in sector as % GDP Source of funds | | R & D in sector as % GDP Performance | | |
|---|---|---|---|---|---|---|---|
| | | | Business | Govt | Business | Govt | Higher education |
| 1  Large R & D performers | 1.17 | 2.47 | 1.35 | 1.16 | 1.53 | 0.36 | 0.36 |
| 2  Medium R & D performers (ex Australia) | 0.89 | 1.65 | 0.85 | 0.67 | 0.98 | 0.20 | 0.33 |
| 3  Small R & D performers | 0.60 | 0.89 | 0.26 | 0.50 | 0.27 | 0.28 | 0.15 |
| Australia | | | | | | | |
| 1968-69 | 0.80 | 1.34 | 0.48 | 0.79 | 0.49 | 0.53 | 0.32 |
| 1973-74 | 0.85 | 1.26 | 0.42 | 0.79 | 0.42 | 0.50 | 0.33 |
| 1976-77 | 0.70 | 1.05 | 0.24 | 0.78 | 0.24 | 0.50 | 0.29 |
| 1978-79 | 0.68 | 1.03 | 0.21 | 0.79 | 0.24 | 0.46 | 0.32 |
| 1981-82 | 0.65 | 0.98 | 0.21 | 0.73 | 0.23 | 0.44 | 0.30 |
| 1983-84 (est.) | n.a. | 0.95 | 0.20 | 0.72 | 0.22 | 0.41 | 0.30 |

1   USA, FR Germany, Japan, UK, France

2   Switzerland, Sweden, Netherlands, Canada, Belgium, Italy, (Australia)

3   Finland, Norway, Austria, Denmark, New Zealand, Ireland, Iceland, Portugal

*Figures are group medians, hence columns do not always add up exactly. Data are latest available for each country (most recent is 1984).

Source:   Department of Science, *Science and Technology Statement 1985–86*, AGPS, Canberra, 1985, p. 45

Table 8 indicates quite clearly Australia's poor performance overall in R & D activity. Our overall level of R & D expenditure is less than 1 per cent of GDP. This compares most unfavourably with large R & D performers who spend almost 2.5 per cent of their GDP on R & D. Even in the medium R & D group, which includes Australia, countries such as Switzerland and Sweden spend over 2.25 per cent of GDP on R & D. Another very disturbing feature is the progressive decline in the last twenty years in our spending on R & D. This has declined from 1.34 per cent of GDP in 1968–69 to 0.95 per cent in 1983–84, a decrease of some 30 per cent. At a time when we should be devoting more of our resources to research and development we are continually devoting less.

Australia compares favourably in the proportion of R & D funds supplied by the government sector. However, we compare very unfavourably in the level of funding provided by the business sector. Table 8 indicates that the business sector in Australia is providing about one-quarter of the level of funding supplied by the business sector in other countries with similar levels of research and development, and less than that provided by the business sector in countries with small overall research and development expenditure. In fact, the only countries in which the business sector provides a smaller percentage of GDP to research and development are New Zealand (0.14), Portugal (0.08) and Iceland (0.04). This is an indefensible situation and is undoubtedly one of our major problems. The business sector in Australia has obviously decided to rely very heavily on imported R & D and has abrogated its responsibility to develop indigenous capabilities in this very fundamental area. Unless this situation is corrected we cannot hope to develop effective indigenous industries which require a high level of sustained quality research and development.

In the past thirty years the greatest increase in per capita GDP has occurred in nations with heavy investment in education and research and development, rather than those with a natural resource base. Japan immediately comes to mind as the leading example. We must at least double our R & D expenditure over the next decade. In doing so we must reverse the present situation so that private-sector funding at least equals that of the government sector. The amount of R & D carried out in tertiary institutions must at least double.

A number of countries have already recognized the need to spend substantial funds in the information technology sector. In the UK for example, in September 1982, government, universities and industries backed the Alvey National Programme for Advanced Information Technology. Alvey's budget is $452 million over five years, although a ten-year programme is envisaged for some aspects such as expert systems.[5] In fact almost $40 million has been allocated specifically for an expert systems research programme, $24 million to be provided by the Alvey directorate and the rest by industry. This is just one of four major enabling technologies which Alvey is pursuing.

In January 1985 ten member countries of the EEC, in collaboration with twelve private European computer and electronics companies, launched the European Strategic Program for Research and Development in Information Technology (ESPRIT). ESPRIT is planned to run for ten years, with an initial budget of $1.3 billion for the first five years incorporating both government and private-sector investment. The programme is focusing its research into five main areas: advanced micro-electronics; advanced information processing; office systems; computing; integrated manufacturing and software technology. The aim of ESPRIT is to create conditions where European industry can jump ahead of US and Japanese competition in the future.

A second European project, called EUREKA (European Co-operative Program in High Technology), was launched in October 1985 by the European Commission and is to co-ordinate the efforts of seventeen private firms. EUREKA has a broad mandate to produce new, successful high-technology products, making use of the relevant research along the way.

Japan has firmly established its world-renowned Institute for New Generation Computer Technology's (ICOT) ten-year national plan, due for completion in 1990. ICOT's estimated overall budget is $A800 million, incorporating considerable private-sector research and financial investment. ICOT is seen by other nations as posing the major threat and challenge in information technology. The US in particular is taking steps to combat the Japanese initiative. The US has strong programmes in advanced information technology, much of which is embodied in defence research projects. There is also considerable research being done in the private sector by large information technology companies and in universities. Australia, however, has no such national programme.

The report by W. D. Scott & Co. in association with Arthur D. Little Inc. on information technology in Australia, produced in July 1984, identified very clearly the need to develop a strategy for Australia to obtain the greatest possible economic benefit from the development of information technology.[6] That report reinforced the need to develop our own information technology to militate against declining relative living standards.

The Scott Little report emphasized the need for Australia to carefully select market niches in information technology. It identified important areas of economic opportunity, including:

- voice recognition and synthesis;
- flat panel displays;
- mass (optical) memories;
- artificial intelligence;
- parallel processing (simultaneous processing of separate logic sequences); and
- image processing by computer.

The report further emphasized the need to develop export markets, and to ensure a greatly increased level of research and development, finance, market access and skilled labour.

# EDUCATION

In any discussion about the development of high-technology industries it becomes very apparent that an essential prerequisite is a well
educated community. One of the most crucial issues confronting us is
our standard of education. As with our standard of living, we have
been lulled into a false sense of complacency. Because the educational
system does change over time, albeit very slowly, and because our
children are learning things at school which we did not, we believe our
educational systems are adequate. In fact, they are grossly inadequate.
In the context of an information society this failure of our educational
systems to cope will prove to be, and has already been in some respects, one of our most debilitating failures. The situation was summed
up very neatly in a survey in the *National Times* (17–23 January 1986)
on career opportunities.

Australia as a nation, by comparison with other industrialised countries, is
woefully under-educated. Many companies have had to resort to recruitment overseas, which is always expensive and often unworkable. They would much rather
hire someone here with the skills they seek, but often this has not been possible
because of Australian students' reluctance to seek higher degrees.

Whilst this comment relates specifically to the post-tertiary level, the
same situation applies at the secondary and tertiary levels. In 1950, 3.5
per cent of the Australian labour force had tertiary qualifications, and
by 1980 this had doubled to 7 per cent. In 1950 Japan had less than 1 per
cent and by 1980 39 per cent, a forty-fold increase.

Senator John Button, speaking on Australia's international compe-
titiveness to the Victorian Economic Society in 1984 said:

Australia has been very badly served by its education system, for example. How can
we become competitive given the quite inadequate performance of this important
sector? If manufacturing has to undergo a painful process of restructuring; if manufacturing has to be competitive; then we must look at other areas where protection
has led to lamentable performance.

The rapidity of technological change in recent years, especially change
driven by the computer, has placed intense pressures on our education systems. How well the systems have responded to those pressures
and how effectively they will respond to future pressures is a vital
issue for debate. Education lies at the heart of the information society,
and a poorly educated public will create, in an information society,
problems that could well have been avoided.

One of our major concerns must be the appallingly low rate of participation in higher education in Australia. In a recent OECD survey
Australia ranked fourteenth in the twenty-three nations listed in full-
time enrolments of people in the 15–19 age group. The percentage of
this age group enrolled in Australia was 45 per cent, compared with 74
per cent in the United States, 71 per cent in Japan, and 65 per cent in
Canada. When we move on to the tertiary level we find Australia's
participation rates are just as low. If we consider the proportion of

17–22-year-olds enrolled in Australia, it is about half that of Japan and one-third that of the United States. The Williams committee report confirmed that while 60 per cent of the 15–19 age group is in the labour force in Australia, the comparable figures are 25 per cent in Japan and 28 per cent in the United States.[7] Consider carefully the impact of those statistics. In Japan and the United States some seven or eight students out of every ten are still in the educational system, whereas in Australia only four out of ten are still at school. Is it any wonder then that we have youth unemployment? We must ask ourselves the question, why have we allowed this to happen? What sort of obstacles are we creating for ourselves tomorrow? In an information society the workforce will need to be better educated, will need to be better able to cope with knowledge-based rather than manual tasks, and yet we are failing to educate adequately for this. Job opportunities are shrinking for those with little education. We are putting out increasing numbers of students who are not just ill-equipped but completely unequipped for the sorts of jobs that are likely to be created in the future.

This brings us to the importance of retraining and continuous education in our system. The day is long since past when the student on leaving school or university will enter a career for life. It is becoming increasingly likely that there will be a need to learn new skills several times during one's working life. This will only be accomplished by continuous education and continuous retraining. Australia's situation in this respect can only be described as completely inadequate. However, we do not want, and we certainly do not need, more of the same. We need to improve the appropriateness of education, recognizing the very different balance of skills required in the future.

One of our fundamental problems is the fear and distrust in the minds of the community, brought about basically by a lack of understanding of technology, particularly computer-based technology. The National Information Technology Council, of which I have been chairman since its inception in 1979, has at least recognized this problem and made some real attempts to address it. Many of the Council's programmes, particularly in the educational arena, have been very successful in helping to enhance understanding of the use of computer-based technology. We have produced projects, publications and activities over the years which have introduced hundreds of thousands of Australians to a better appreciation and understanding of information technology.

We cannot overlook the importance of an understanding throughout the community of the benefits of new technologies applied to existing processes. For example, studies by the South Australian Technological Change Council and the Technological Change Committee of the Australian Science and Technology Council (ASTEC) have found that the major barrier to the application of micro-electronic techniques in Australian industry is a lack of tradespeople, technicians, engineers and managers who have an appreciation of contemporary technology.

We see many manifestations of this. For example, in terms of patents taken out world-wide each year per million people, Australia ranks eighteenth out of twenty-four technologically advanced nations.

A number of countries have already taken a lead in recognizing education and training in micro-electronics as a key to their future economic strategy. In Singapore, for example, we see a positive government initiative introduced some two years ago to produce over the next few years 700 computer science graduates per year. This is a country with a population about the same as the city of Melbourne. When we compare that to the annual output of similar graduates in Australia, of some 1200–1500 per year, it underlines the lack of planning in Australia in this direction. This is not the worst of it, however. Our tertiary institutions, particularly the universities, are imposing (or being forced to impose) increasingly stringent quotas in disciplines such as computer science, information processing and so on. In 1984, for example, Sydney University was forced, for the first time, to impose quotas in computer science. How do we reconcile this ridiculous situation with the need to prepare for an information society? How do we reconcile these decisions with the decisions we see being taken by our neighbours and in other industrialized nations?

When we speak of the balance of skills required, it is interesting to look at the relevant proportion of professional groups in the United States, Japan and Australia. The United States has twenty lawyers for every 10 000 of population, Japan has one and Australia has two. The United States has forty accountants for every 10 000 of population, Japan has three and Australia has twenty-two. The most interesting comparison is for scientists and engineers, where the US has seventy per 10 000 of population, Australia has forty-six and Japan has 400. Would it be reasonable to suggest that this correlates very closely with the success Japan has had in developing high technologies in recent years? To achieve the proper balance of skills it is essential that we recognize the central relationship between human resource development and the effective use of technology. Whether the information society will be beneficial or not will depend on the adequacy of our human resources.

## SETTING NATIONAL GOALS

One of the major hurdles we face is that we have no clear national idea of what we want to achieve. We must formulate a set of national goals if we hope to succeed. There are many examples of other countries who have addressed this issue. Singapore, Japan, Sweden, the United Kingdom, West Germany, France and others have well-developed plans, objectives and strategies to achieve those objectives. We have to shake off the 'lucky country' syndrome and realize that luck has nothing at all to do with our future situation. We can no longer rely on natural resources and protected industries to fuel our future economic growth. We must develop, for example, a national information policy, a framework within which plans and policies can be formulated and action taken, a plan which is comprehensive, but sensitive in response to new technologies and their implications.

There are several aspects of government policies and mechanisms which are relevant to developing indigenous industries in information technology. Government procurement is particularly important, as governments (at all levels) are users of information technology; computer systems and telecommunications, in particular, are very extensively used in government. Hand in hand with these go maintenance and other ancillary services. Also associated with government procurement are preferences extended to Australian-made goods, by way of a quantum preference or by way of other support mechanisms. Government plays a particularly important role in the funding of R & D. Offsets are another mechanism already in use for increasing industry capabilities and assisting Australian manufacturers in developing local industries. Other measures such as tariffs, export incentive schemes, subsidies of one kind or another, grants, incentives, provision or support of venture capital, taxation concessions and similar measures can all be applied in particular circumstances to help Australian manufacturers to compete or develop new markets. They must be used judiciously, however, to help promote efficient competition and not merely support inefficient operations.

The Scott Little report estimated that the most that could be expected if current conditions were to continue would be a growth in annual Australian information technology-related production from its 1982 level of $1.4 billion to about $2.9 billion by 1992. However, its authors believed that local production could be stimulated to produce information technology products and services valued at $5–$6 billion by 1992—in other words, that output could be at least doubled. They also estimated that revenues of some $3 billion could be gained by 1992 from the export of selected Australian information technology products and services to the United States and Europe. They also believed it would be feasible for Australia to establish itself as a leading source of information technology expertise for the developing countries of the Asia–Pacific region in the 1990s and beyond.[8] To achieve these sorts of goals, however, there must be positive action to stimulate research and development, stimulate private enterprise growth in the information technology sector, stimulate exports, and encourage the formation of larger, more viable business units. There must be programmes of support for innovation.

We cannot, and should not, enter the market for mass-produced mainframe items. We must target specific markets such as special-purpose products (the VLSI plant in Adelaide is a good example of this), clearly differentiated products, systems with high value-added content, and particularly systems of special relevance to developing nations. Australia should be aiming to have a significant presence in the South-East Asian area. The potential growth is enormous.

In view of the importance of information technology, and the information industry in general, in terms of employment, export markets, national self-sufficiency, strategic defence capability and industry development, the time is appropriate to have a Minister for Information Technology, as some other countries already do, to focus resources and attention on this vital area. Our underlying attitude to what we are capable of achieving must change. We are not too small, we are not geographically isolated, we have the skills, we have the capacity. What we do not have is the belief in ourselves that as individuals and as a nation we can effectively compete and lead in the field of information technology. We must adopt a positive attitude that we are going to be leaders in information technology, and we have to put into place the necessary infrastructure, educational, economic, financial and attitudinal, that will enable us to achieve these goals. Without this basic belief in ourselves, and a goal to aim at, we will continue to wallow in a sea of indecision and inaction, and we will continue to see our standard of living decline and our economic well-being rapidly deteriorating.

# PART II

# Information, Citizens and Social Policy

Information, Citizens and
Social Policy

# CHAPTER 5

# THE IMPACT OF TECHNOLOGY ON COMMUNITY INFORMATION PROCESSES

## John Burke

People will not be able to get their due as citizens of present day society unless they have continuous access to the information which will guide them through it, and where necessary the advice to help them translate that information into effective action; and unless they get their due they are unlikely to recognise the reciprocal obligation that all citizens have to society.

National Consumer Council of the United Kingdom[1]

Will the advent of an 'information society' improve the prospects of individuals obtaining community information of the kind described in the quotation? Will the processes through which individuals most effectively obtain such information be supported?

In considering the potential impact of the development of an 'information society' on community information processes, we first need an understanding of terms and of the kinds of processes to which we are referring.

## WHAT IS MEANT BY AN 'INFORMATION SOCIETY'?

In an important sense all societies are information societies. Information is critical to individual and social action: without patterns of information flow it is difficult to see that anything that can be described as a 'society' can be said to exist. What new characteristics of society, then, are denoted by the term 'information society'? There appear to be two: the extensive application of information technology, and an increased emphasis placed on *formal* information provision within the economy of the society.

It is useful to be aware that this 'new' concept of an information society is almost always used without an appreciation of the natural processes of information exchange within a society, primarily through people talking to one another. This perspective underlies the discussion paper 'A National Information Policy for Australia', published by the Department of Science in 1985, which sees us as being involved in a 'process of transition to a society based primarily on information exchange and heavily dependent on information technology'.[2]

In this chapter the impact of the 'information society' will be considered primarily in terms of the applications of information technology; but it must be clearly understood that this leaves out a very important dimension of information exchange.

## WHAT ARE 'COMMUNITY INFORMATION PROCESSES'?

'Community information' can be defined as information that is necessary for individuals or groups to utilize effectively the resources of their society. This information may range from the detail of the neighbourhood or municipality to the nationally common material of pensions, benefits, passport procedures, etc. It may include information about physical resources (halls, chairs, typewriters, etc.) and human resources (skills, interests of individuals) in a local community; activities and services of local organizations, both transient and long-term; current issues in the community; local government regulations and services; activities and services of regional, State and Federal organizations; State and Federal government regulations, guidelines and services; rights of individuals and how to exercise them; and guidelines and procedural information for pursuing particular actions. From this point of view, community information is broader than 'community services information', which is information about services provided by government and other agencies, although information about such services is a significant component.

Much of community information as defined above is clearly the stuff of personal communication—'I think you could get Sickness Benefit, have you tried DSS?' or 'I heard so-and-so is interested in forming a playgroup in the church, why don't you talk to her?'. This is how most people obtain this kind of information; from friends, family, significant other people, through informal processes.[3] These processes embrace networks of personal contacts, chains of people through whom information is disseminated, links to people who are known to know about certain areas or able to link to others who do know. The strength, accessibility and comprehensiveness of such networks are prerequisites for a cohesive community.

There is nothing planned about this dimension of community information processes. There is also, however, a dimension of formal services, of structured, intentional provision of information. Many organizations participate in one way or another, including government agencies, libraries, general community organizations, and special-interest organizations (with a focus on, for example, issues affecting women, disabled people or ethnic groups). These formal services have differing objectives; some providing information about a particular set of services, others providing information for the use of specific groups, others being concerned with providing general access to the broad range of community information. There are relatively few organizations that have such objectives as their primary focus. The Citizens Advice Bureau movement in Victoria is one of the better developed, with sixty-four local bureaus with common standards, policies, training and other support structures. As an example of the practical impact of such a service, these bureaus deal with over 200 000 enquiries a year, ranging from 700 to 1000 in smaller bureaus to over 20 000 in the busiest. The major categories of these enquiries are legal (20 per cent), community organizations (18 per cent) and personal and family matters (15 per cent). In the United Kingdom the longer-established CAB movement has over 900 bureaus dealing with about four million enquiries per year. Services of this type—the formal, though not highly developed, social structures through which community information is disseminated—can extend the quality and scope of information available through personal networks, by providing access to information for people whose networks are restricted, making available complex information and information which changes frequently.

In addition to these formal services and informal processes, the mass media are a third major component in community information processes, often as a channel for dissemination of information by other organizations. They offer a transient form of information dissemination, usually with little or no capacity to respond to individual needs. Nevertheless, they are clearly significant in their breadth of contact with members of society, and perhaps most useful in developing an initial awareness of the availability of further information, and of sources through which this can be obtained.

## ISSUES IN THE FUTURE DEVELOPMENT OF COMMUNITY INFORMATION SERVICES

Among the issues that present experience throws up for consideration are:

1 Resourcing    The basic requirements of community information services are physical, human and financial resources. To put larger plans in context, more than half of the sixty-four Victorian CABs mentioned above operate on a budget of less than $5000 a year; a level of income on which they cannot contemplate paid part-time administration or co-ordination, the purchase of a photocopier, or an effective budget allocation for paid publicity. (They can only function because of the contributions of over 2000 volunteers throughout the State.)

2 Examination of the appropriateness of different models    At least two broad models of information services are being pursued. One may be referred to as a 'direct access' or 'self-service' model, where an information file is made available without any intermediary; an

enquirer is presumed able to determine his or her need and to select from the file appropriately. The other may be referred to as a 'personal assistance' model in which people are helped to determine their information need, to identify information relevant to that need, and to establish a preferred course of action. The 'direct access' model is likely to be most effective with people of higher education and socio-economic status. The 'personal assistance' model has a greater apparent affinity with the natural processes of acquisition of information through personal networks. Some research indicates the preference of lower socio-economic groups for personal assistance.[4]

While these are the primary models for formal information services, other less formal approaches are also being explored. These include the establishment of a secondary information function in an activist or special-interest community organization, and the linking of people to other networks through learning exchanges or other means.

*3 Access and equity issues*    Fundamental to the development of community information services should be a principle of universal access to relevant information. If this principle is to be followed, services must allow for differentials in the information-seeking public. Do people know about the services? Would everyone feel free to use them, or are there invisible barriers? Are they easy to get to? Are non-English-speaking people catered for? Present community information services are probably not giving enough attention to these important questions.

*4 Data management*    Community information services have data management requirements. A Victorian CAB, for example, may have a card file of 3000 to 4000 items, of which half may be Statewide information and the remainder local. In addition, it maintains more detailed information in hanging files and collections of directories, pamphlets, etc. However, it is probable that 80 per cent of bureaus would search their files less than twenty times a day. In other words, present community information services may have moderate-size files, but their comparatively limited access-requirements at present are not such as to require other data management approaches.[5]

Community information services probably experience greater difficulty in updating, rather than storing, their data. In Victoria, as in most States, maintenance of Statewide information—which should be provided to local information services in some common format—is inadequate. At the local level the updating task is very labour-intensive, usually requiring extensive telephone or other personal contact to establish the necessary details.

*5 Examination of information needs and targeting of special groups*    There is a lack of sophistication in the planning of community information services. For example, municipal officers might well know how to identify needs for child care and plan appropriate strategies for meeting these; they are most unlikely to have any comparable skills in respect of the less tangible information needs of the community.

6 Interaction of formal services and informal processes    If most people obtain information through informal processes, how can formal services feed in to these processes? How can the quality of information flowing through personal networks be improved? Is this primarily a matter of using the media? How can access to networks be improved for individuals? Are people necessarily restricted to the networks of their sub-culture? Can formal services assist in linking people into other networks? How can knowledge of the existence of useful formal services be embedded in the personal networks?

There are two broad observations I would make from examination of these issues. First, we know very little about how community information processes work or how to evaluate the effectiveness of information services—there are many more questions than answers about the most productive approach to follow. Second, it is important to draw distinctions between *data provision*—the maintenance and presentation of recorded information and *information access*—the means by which people obtain information appropriate for their purposes. Of these, the access component has the higher priority for resourcing and investigation.

## IMPACTS

Given the above as a broad-brush view of the field of community information and the developmental issues confronting it, what is the relevance of the development of an 'information society'? What may be the impact of a greater interest in the information component of society, and of increasing application of information technology? The answer is probably that it depends on how these developments are handled.

An increased interest in the information component of society will presumably be revealed through an increasing attention to policy development and resourcing of formal information services. The simplest approach is to apply increased resources to the direct dissemination of information about community services, particularly those provided by Federal and State governments. (At its coarsest, this approach reduces to a media blitz.) But this will not work unless the resourcing is based on an understanding of the processes by which people obtain information. Constructive proposals were developed in 1986 at an interstate conference of community information providers, for consideration as part of national information policy development.[6]

If we now turn to the question of the impact of information technology we need first to clarify some fundamental matters of orientation. Should we be examining this question in terms of a possible
complete shift in paradigm? Will an increased application of information technology lead to completely new modes of exchange of information and if so, will they dominate over old modes? Or can the
question be examined from the perspective of existing structures?

One very powerful view in society embraces the former perspective, and it is usually from this perspective that the concept of an
'information society' is addressed. It is usually a grand image which
sees the pursuit of technology-based procedures as the underpinning
of future development. This is a view that may arise from a sense of
historical inevitability of fundamental change through technological
development, it may be embraced on the basis of assumption or belief,
or it may be a perceptive extrapolation of existing development. On
each of the first two bases it is questionable; the latter may involve
greater foresight than those of us who are sceptical will at present
admit.

There is nothing inevitable about the details or effects of technological change. While there may be powerful forces directed at
supporting particular changes—through skilful marketing and the
convictions of many people in positions of social power—and these
forces may indeed have effect regardless of the actual value of the
change, it will not always happen that the far-reaching claims for new
applications of technology will be realized. A significant example is
the failure of computer applications in education to achieve the
extravagant claims made for them in the 1960s, when computer-
assisted and computer-managed instruction was heralded as a revolution in educational processes, providing immediate access to all the
world's knowledge in ways particularly appropriate to individual students and without the necessity for a teacher. The reality of these
applications was significantly different from this prediction, and computers are now essentially limited to an ancillary role in the learning
process.

There are reasons for the failure of specific technological developments. While the proponents of such change will frequently attribute
failure to the conservatism of the people involved (e.g. teachers), the
reasons are, I believe, far more profound and have to do with the fundamental limitations of the technology proposed. These limitations
are particularly clear in the applications of computer-based technologies to interactive human activities. Computers are suited to solving well-defined problems that can be rendered in rational terms. Few
complex human situations can be presented in this way, entailing as
they do many variables such as elements of intuition, personal history,
context of immediate experience, and interpersonal dynamics. Computer-based technologies simply cannot embrace this complexity, nor
can they cope with the necessary free-form natural language processes. They become established to deal with a limited, essentially

cognitive abstraction expressed in terms they can manage. If this inadequacy and the consequent disregard of the actualities of human interactions are of considerable significance but the developments are nevertheless forced through the societal power structures, limiting processes will then become embedded in the social structure—and create more of Leunig's cartoon men watching the moon on TV when it is visible through the open window.

There are, then, doubts about not only the inevitability of technological change but also the value and consequences of such change. In the early 1970s the Priorities Review Staff's document *Goals and Strategies* recognized this quite clearly, saying:

We must try to ensure that society can supply itself with information in the most honest and efficient way and never lose sight of the fact that information policy is *in the last analysis about communications between people and not about marvels of technique.* The choices we make, even though they appear merely choices of technologies, will affect not only the nature of the information communicated but even the type of people we are. In this field, the future is crowding in on us.[7] (my emphasis)

Joseph Weizenbaum, creator of the interactive computer counselling program Eliza and subsequently confirmed critic of artificial intelligence developments, put it another way:

We have permitted technological metaphors, and technique itself, to so thoroughly pervade our thought processes that we have finally abdicated to technology the very duty to formulate questions. Thus sensible men correctly perceive that large data banks and enormous networks of computers threaten man. But they leave it to technology to formulate the corresponding question. Where a simple man might ask: 'Do we need these things?', technology asks 'What electronic wizardry will make them safe?' Where a simple man will ask 'Is it good?', technology asks, 'Will it work?'. Thus science, even wisdom, becomes what technology and most of all computers can handle . . .[8]

The field of community information might be seen now to be in a similar situation to that of education in the 1960s. The claims being made for the potential of technological applications are remarkably similar, and in my view no more soundly based. The new modes of information acquisition which are proposed usually involve the utilization of large data bases with direct access through keyboard and screen terminal; videotex systems are examples of this approach which are now being promoted heavily.

In terms of the issues considered earlier these proposals promote a 'direct access' model, with consequent limitations on the range of people likely to utilize them. Originating as they usually do out of a technocratic sub-culture, they need to assume that all people will have equal facility with new technology. Often they go further and suggest that the widespread development of technological capability will in fact cause such systems to provide greater access to information. This seems unlikely, although the active developments in this area in respect particularly of young people indicate that this is a moot point, and clearly the extent to which such systems extend effective access and promote greater equity is worth close scrutiny.

These systems will, however, consume considerable resources in a scarce resource sector. If we conclude that they are neither inevitable nor clearly so intrinsically desirable as to be the cornerstone of social policy, they should—at least insofar as their development is subject to social policy decisions rather than the free market—be evaluated by comparison with other strategies for meeting the developmental needs of community information processes. One of the greatest difficulties in the examination of technological possibilities is that this comparison usually does not occur. The 'technological determinist' perspective tends to allow only for the examination of social change from the point of view of technological capacity, and does not allow for the definition of social goals and needs, the examination of alternative strategies for meeting these, and the recognition that there are significant social policy questions involved in the choices of resourcing these alternative strategies. These general issues are clearly mirrored in the field of community information.

If we forgo the grand image of the technologically-based information society, we can look at the present and potential applications of information technology in the context of the structures, processes and issues presented in the earlier analysis in this chapter. In practice we find other instances of technocratic zeal overriding careful examination of needs, alternative strategies, and possible impacts of technological developments; in general there is a need in the community service sector for a greater capacity to systematically analyse objectives, strategies, and the role and impacts of technology in relation to these.[9]

However, when all the needs for caution are taken into account and the clear view of practitioners that any useful developments must enhance, rather than replace, 'personal assistance' models of information acquisition is recognized, there are significant applications of information technology which are seen to have current or potential merit.

These applications particularly relate to the management of large data bases, usually at the state or regional level, from which hard copy or screen-based data can be supplied to intermediaries assisting enquirers, and the distribution of data through networks of organizational or other contact points primarily at local or regional levels. Access and equity are thus strengthened through the co-operative work of a number of different services and individuals who may provide greater psychological or geographic ease of contact for particular persons or groups. Information technology may support such developments, but it is still not the core of the process, which is a co-operative human interaction based on shared perspectives of needs.

These and other applications need to be monitored so that their real benefits and impacts can be determined and so that expensive but inadequate systems do not become embedded. Information technology may play a major role in supporting important developments in the community information area, although the focus of applications lies mostly in supporting the data provision component of services rather than the more difficult and higher-priority issues in the area of ensuring access to personally relevant information.

## CONCLUSION

Most people gain information through personal, informal channels. Much of this information is inaccurate and inadequate. People frequently fail to obtain adequate information because of the limitations of their own networks and because they do not feel formal services are relevant or accessible. How can formal, planned activities overcome these deficiencies?

It is from the detailed examination of this perspective that the most productive developments in community information are likely to occur. The questions arising are more in the realm of anthropology—in developing a greater understanding of the natural processes of information acquisition and usage—and of sociology—in examining the impediments to obtaining access to formal information provision—than in the realm of technology. While there are applications of information technology which promise support for useful developments, the new concept of a technologically-based 'information society' pays little if any regard to the fundamental issues. It may be embraced to the detriment of real social progress.

# CHAPTER 6

# BRAVE NEW WIRED WORLD

## Marie Keir

## A TASTE OF THE FUTURE?

*Record Sheet*    CONFIDENTIAL    11 June 1986

*Subject:*
Leah Jane Georgenson, 5A Grant Street, Macandrew Bay, NSW.
Female, age 37, divorced, lawyer.

*Purchases*
The Australian Financial Review, 70c; Breakfast, Tiffany's,
$5.75; Petrol, BP Self-Serve, Glenfalloch, $15.00; Phone, (03
12 3489), $4.56; Lunch, Fed Up, $35.45; Autobank withdrawal,
Glenfalloch, $150.00; Shirt, Plume, $74.99; Phone (02 63 9006)
20c; Phone (09 44 3771), $12.56; Dimple Haig, Ballantynes Drive-
In Liquor Store, $27.50.[1]

In July 1986, the major trading banks agreed over the future of Bank-
card, the most popular credit card in Australia. The rules covering the
use of the card were to be changed to allow it to be used as both a credit
and a debit card. The banks also plan to link their EFTPOS (electronic
funds transfer at the point of sale) systems so that any card issued by
the banks within the agreement can be used at any retailers who have
installed an EFTPOS terminal. By early 1988, anyone with a bank-
issued plastic card will be able to shop electronically at any store with
an appropriate terminal and will be given the choice of whether the
purchase is made by debit or credit.[2] The change will effectively turn
the older type of credit card into an electronic cheque book as well and
will make plastic cards more attractive to many people. The older
paper-based credit cards will probably be quickly phased out, leaving
the plastic card and cash (to a more limited extent) the most common
ways of paying for purchases.

Australia is one of the first countries in the world to have a nation-
wide network for electronic funds transfer at the point of sale. The
system is still in its beginning stages, but its introduction and use show

features that are common to any computerized information system, for that is what money is becoming: high-velocity information. Very soon the list of purchases recorded for the fictional Leah Jane Georgenson may be common practice, and an apparently convenient one. However, we need to consider in some detail what effects cashless payments will have on Australian society. To do this we need first to understand what EFTPOS is, why it has been introduced, and the advantages and disadvantages it brings us.

## PRESSURES TO INTRODUCE ELECTRONIC FUNDS TRANSFERS

Over the past few decades, the banking and retail industries, both here and abroad, have automated many of their routine information-processing activities in attempts to lessen their cost increases.[3]. Banks, credit unions and building societies have attracted a large increase in accounts; there has therefore been growth in the paper-processing involved in servicing deposits and withdrawals. The use of plastic cards has been encouraged to reduce the volume of paper transactions. At the same time, automation has enabled banks to increase their range of customer services without increasing their staff numbers. Many of these new services, such as the installation of automatic teller machines (ATMs), rely on customer self-service rather than on personal attention from bank staff. Numbers of other comparable services, including credit authorization and credit contracts, are expected to be automated soon, as costs continue to rise.

Although retailing is more diverse than banking, the stores with a high-volume low-value turnover, petrol stations and chains of small specialist stores have been those most affected by the recent changes, which have also been in response to the need to hold costs in a fiercely competitive retail environment. EFTPOS is one of the most recent additions to the battery of automation which exists in the banking and retail industries.

## EFTPOS IN AUSTRALIA

EFTPOS is the next step in the progression towards a less-cash, fewer-cheques society which began over two decades ago with the electronic transfer of money between banks. These exchanges were, on the whole, invisible to customers, who still dealt with bank tellers over a counter. The second stage of bank computerization was introduced by the installation of automatic teller machines in the late 1970s, which enabled remote-access processing of funds by banks and which allowed account-holders to withdraw money at an ATM terminal during or outside bank hours of work. Australians rapidly became relatively heavy users of these computerized facilities for cash withdrawals.

Probably heartened by the success of ATMs, a number of financial institutions began shortly afterwards to experiment with EFTPOS in retail stores and petrol stations. In 1982 a credit union in South Australia began an EFTPOS trial with G. J. Coles. In early 1984, the Australian Bankers' Association agreed to the establishment of an EFT clearing house for point of sale transactions. At about the same time, credit unions and building societies began operating a shared network of ATMs which would accept cards from all network participants.

The Standards Association of Australia set up an EFT working party to establish the standards that would enable any institution to develop an EFT system that was fully compatible with others in Australia. The working party was also responsible for setting national standards for terminals, switching facilities and plastic cards.

The four major banks set up a pilot EFTPOS scheme which was well established by early 1985, with about twenty major retailers taking cards from one of the four banks for EFTPOS payments. Subsequently Coles Myer negotiated with the Bank of America, one of the foreign banks now operating in Australia, to operate in-store banking facilities. An estimated 4000 EFTPOS terminals were to be installed in retail stores by the end of 1985.

## HOW EFTPOS WORKS

Banks, credit unions or building societies provide approved account-holders with a plastic card they can use to make purchases in shops with EFTPOS facilities. Card-holders take what they wish to buy to the point of sale, the shop counter. The shop assistant calculates the price of the purchase, takes the customer's card and passes it through a card-reader on the point of sale terminal which is part of an electronic cash register. The action triggers a message which is sent, for example, through Telecom's network, via a gateway to the card-issuing institution. At the same time, customers 'sign' an authorization for the payment by entering their personal identification numbers (PINs), known only to them, into a hand-held pad, similar in appearance to a calculator. When this electronic signature is received by the financial institution's computer, a message is sent back to the customer and the shop assistant saying whether or not the payment can be made. The message is usually in the form of 'approved', or 'Please contact your bank' if there are insufficient funds in the customer's account to cover the purchase price. The sale slip is printed by the store's cash register and given to the customer to record the purchase. The customer's account at the bank is debited with the amount of the purchase, which is deposited in the retailer's account as soon as possible. The whole process should take between fifteen and twenty seconds, about the same time it takes to pay by cash. As was mentioned earlier, electronic debits of this kind are an electronic parallel to paying by cheque.

Leah Jane Georgenson could be any one of us, now or in the near future. She holds a plastic card with which she pays for almost everything she buys. Cash is used sparingly. Leah Jane makes purchases by serving herself at the petrol station. She fills the petrol tank and swipes her card through the terminal beside the pump to pay for it without the need for an attendant. In the supermarket she collects her own groceries and could pay for them by passing them over the scanner which records items and prices before using the EFTPOS terminal and PIN pad to pay. The checkout counter assistant is there mainly for security reasons, rather than for customer service. Leah Jane rarely enters her bank, as she is able to make deposits and withdrawals on her own at an ATM and her pay is directly credited to her bank account.

## MORE SELF-SERVICE—FEWER EMPLOYMENT OPPORTUNITIES?

The use of EFTPOS and ATMs show very clearly the advantages and disadvantages of the growing use of computers in our society. One of the clear lessons, even from the short example above, is that their effects are often contradictory; both good and bad.

We are becoming a more self-service society. We can help ourselves to all kinds of services by using computer terminals. We can shop from home through Viatel, do our banking and bill-paying from home using Telebank, as well as carry out the other activities just mentioned. This has the advantage of avoiding cost increases that banks and retailers might otherwise pass on to customers. Electronic payments and self-service are cheaper than processing cash and paper money and employing larger numbers of staff for customer assistance. Moreover, it is often more convenient for us to help ourselves to goods and services, as it saves time and can be done at hours which may not fall in with bank and shop working time. However, there should be the choice of personal service for those who are unfamiliar with the skills needed or who have a handicap of some kind that precludes them from easily carrying out the necessary functions themselves.

There is another side to the changes described here. A recent Japanese report reviewing micro-electronics noted changes in the number of available jobs and in the type of work that people do when various computerized systems have been introduced.[4] It is not entirely accurate to blame computers alone for job losses, for alterations to the nature of work, and other appreciable social changes. These events often occur as a result of an accumulation of technologies which are introduced in response to economic pressures such as fiercer international competition. The increasing automation of the retail sector, for example, has encompassed the introduction of computers for accounting purposes, electronic scanning and weighing machines, electronic cash registers and point-of-sale terminals. The innovations have resulted, in combination with other trends, in fewer, larger stores, the increased customer self-service we are familiar with, a decline in small family businesses, and changes in floor display, payout and payment areas. These changes have been accompanied by the increasing employment of part-time and casual workers—a trend sometimes referred to as the casualization of work.

Unions in both industries affected have noted a number of concerns they feel over what has accompanied the technological changes of the past few years, including EFT and EFTPOS. Among the points they raise are that:

• the new systems are predominantly process- rather than product-based, and process changes are characteristically labour-saving;
• banking and retailing are beginning to overlap, with the dispersal of banking services into stores, thus potentially removing some work from bank employees;
• there is a declining number of jobs available to school leavers, who in the past had a comparatively large number of employment opportunities in banking, insurance and general clerical occupations;
• employment opportunities in the increased services offered by banks have to be set against the increasing competition among banks, travel agents, insurance companies and even retailers. Services of these kinds might soon reach saturation point and would be shared out among these industries, offering steady or decreasing job opportunities in banking, not the growth predicted by the Australian Bankers' Association;
• retail employment in stores with a high-volume low-value turnover have already been reduced to a minimum and staff numbers are unlikely to fall further unless cost pressures change;
• there is difficulty in defining bank employment now that banks are increasing their range of services.

The Australian Bankers' Association has taken issue with the forecast of possible staff reductions in banking, noting that employment in the industry has grown over the past two decades. They have not, however, predicted that this employment growth would continue. The private banks have given an undertaking that they will not retrench staff in the foreseeable future but, as in retailing, this could change if cost pressures increase markedly.

Not only is it difficult to be optimistic about the direct and indirect effect of computers on employment, it is also appropriate to note their influence on the types of work carried out in banks and retail stores.

## INCREASED AUTOMATION OF ROUTINE WORK— LESS WORK VARIETY?

Computers are often used to carry out the more tedious routine work. In banks and stores automation is reducing the drudgery of carrying out myriads of arithmetical calculations. However, despite such benefits as these, the Shop Distributive and Allied Employees' Association (SDA) is concerned that retail automation will eventually mean that staff are restricted to a small number of retail operations which will reduce their skills and therefore make staff members more readily interchangeable. If this degree of compartmentalization occurs, then staff will need less training and will be more easily replaced by part-time or casual workers. In a submission to the Senate Standing Committee Inquiry into New Technology and Employment, the Australian Bank Employees' Union (ABEU) noted parallel developments in banking which have altered the nature of clerical work, in some instances reducing the skills needed by employees. Bank work appears to be polarizing into two types of jobs: those which do not require a high level of skill and which are readily interchangeable, and those highly skilled jobs of a specialist nature which require tertiary training.

## MORE VARIED SERVICES—LESS INDIVIDUAL ATTENTION?

Consumers are affected as directly as banking and retail employees. Computers offer consumers a greater range of services, for example through the introduction of ATMs, which have provided out-of-hours cash withdrawals, and of EFTPOS which, at present, adds to the number of ways in which they can make payments. However, the costs could be in greater standardization, not only of work, as has been described, but in the way in which people must behave to take advantage of the services.

To illustrate, it is likely that banks will soon introduce a program to be used by people seeking a personal loan. Instead of seeking an appointment with a bank official, the person wanting credit will use a terminal to answer a number of questions. When the answers to these have been processed, the loan will be approved, if the right combination of facts about the applicant emerges. As a step in this direction, the ANZ Bank has installed a new-style ATM in a Melbourne suburb. The ATM will operate as an automated bank branch without staff and will provide these services: marketing and advertising of new accounts; brokerage services; loans; investments; the calculation of loan costs; certificates of deposits and travel services.[5]

Seeking loans in this way will be little different from filling in forms when we apply for a credit card or a mortgage. These already raise difficulties in that individual treatment is less possible under the rigid formulae banks impose. If the applicant does not fit the profile set down by the bank, an application is likely to be unsuccessful. The extension of applications for credit cards and personal loans to computers, however, intensifies the standardization of treatment that already exists. Moreover, when ATMs do not operate as they should there may be difficulties in contacting a bank employee to discover what went wrong, how a successful application can be made and so on.

This separation from other people caused by the use of computers will be returned to later.

The advantage of standardization is that the services are likely to be available at any place and at any time. It is already possible, for example, for visiting Americans to use some plastic cards in Australia at ATMs to draw on their US bank accounts.

## MORE VARIED SERVICES—MORE CONVERGENCE OF WORK?

The different services offered by computers obviously affect us both as consumers and as workers. Returning to the subject of work, it is already clear that retail stores have taken over some banking functions, as many of them agree to allow customers to make cash withdrawals by using their EFTPOS cards. Thus retailers are beginning to compete, not only with each other in the provision of services, but also with banks. Indeed, as so much work these days depends on information processing of one type or another, the boundaries between work of various kinds is blurring. Is a checkout operator who gives a customer $150 cash, which has been debited to the customer's bank account by using EFTPOS, a shop assistant or a bank teller at that moment? Is a bank officer who deals with travel arrangements really a travel agent?

Another trend that has occurred is that retail automation has been used to centralize decision-making in large firms, restricting it to the head office, which takes over a number of functions previously carried out in branches. This convergence of work from many places to one central point, means that many head offices carry out accounting, stock control, ordering and purchasing, all of which involve information collection, storage and processing.

These trends raise questions about the suitability of the present union structures for representing their members and for consulting over changes. Should unions have to consult with each other more as work becomes less easily identifiable as, for example, banking or retailing? Whom should employers consult when changes they have in mind affect people outside the unions they may have dealt with in the past?

## MORE SERVICES—INCREASED PERSONAL LIABILITY?

Union–employer relationships are often set down in legal form. The same applies to the contractual relationships that exist between banks and their account-holders; between retailers and their customers. Rights and responsibilities of both parties in the past have been set down by law and have been fairly well known. When plastic debit cards were introduced, the initial terms and conditions of use set down by banks for card-holders were unclear, difficult to obtain and inconsistent. The liability of banks for lost funds varied. Liability apparently moved from a reasonably equal distribution between banks and their clients to a situation where clients held a great deal more responsibility for loss or error.

After discussion with government departments and consumer organizations, the banks are voluntarily altering the original terms and conditions of use to share liability more fairly. However, the example of plastic cards serves to illustrate the difficulties in allocating responsibility for loss and error when computerized systems fail to operate or become the object of crime.

## FASTER SERVICE—LESS CONTROL?

There are also issues emerging from international data flows. At the institutional level, increased computer power has increased both the speed and volume of financial transactions among banks and financial markets around the world. For example, the Reuter Money Dealing Service had 1200 users, between 2500 and 3000 terminals, and was averaging 50 000 conversations involving transactions each day in early 1986. In mid–1985, dealings through two of the major networks totalled approximately US$600 billion daily. The expectation that funds will be turned over quickly has reached the point where complaints are made when a person's capital has been invested and reinvested only seven or eight times in one day.

A concern emerging from the increased speed and volume of international funds transfers is that market instabilities will be caused. As yet the patterns are inadequately understood. Another concern is that many countries will lose control of the mechanisms that govern their currencies. Then there is the real fear that a shift in financial volumes could allow the world's largest banks to lose the equivalent of a moderate-sized country's gross domestic product. If this happened, the bank would be likely to fail, with severe international repercussions.[6] The world financial markets do not normally impinge on many of us as individuals, but their instability or failure could cause social as well as economic havoc.

## MORE INFORMATION—LESS PRIVACY?

Information held in data banks is particularly vulnerable to misuse. So far the discussion has focused on the effects of EFTPOS as a form of payment. Its capacity to collect, store and process personal information about individuals has other implications.

The brief illustration at the beginning of the chapter is based on a system devised in the United States in 1975, when a firm of consultants was asked to design a system for the unobtrusive surveillance of all citizens. What the firm provided was a system very similar to EFTPOS. Everyone would be given a plastic card to use for payment of goods and services. The data produced by the sale would be stored in the data bases of a number of computers, all part of a network, and the information analysed. Not only would it be possible to print out details of individual purchases, as we saw at the beginning of the chapter, it would also be feasible to analyse the data, cross-check between people and to draw certain conclusions. An analysis of Leah Jane Georgenson's transactions for 11 June 1986 could therefore read:

*Computer Analysis*

Owns shares (90% probability);

Croissants for breakfast five days a week—probably overweight; also drinks two cups of coffee—if this pattern continues all day, caffeine intake is too high;

Bought $15.00 of petrol. Subject owns Honda Civic. So far this week has bought $20.00 worth of petrol. Means significantly more driving than required to travel to and from work.

Bought petrol at 8.25, four kilometres from work. Subject probably late for work. Third such occurrence this week.

Phone 03 12 3489 belongs to a person who has been convicted of drunk-driving in Victoria. The person is not a client of the firm the subject works for.

Entertained a person for lunch. Bought a Fumé Blanc.

Withdrew $150.00 cash. Very unusual, since most purchases can be made using the combined debit/credit card subject holds. Cash usually is withdrawn for illegal purposes or for those the subject does not want recorded.

Shirt not brother's or father's size.

Phone 02 63 9006 belongs to a hairdresser. Subject due for regular hairstyling and tint.

Phone 09 44 3771 belongs to a sister.

Purchased Dimple Haig. Does not usually spend this amount on a bottle of whisky. May intend entertaining visitors (75% probability; 25%, celebration of some kind). Subject left work at 4.30 p.m. as she bought whisky one kilometre from her job at 4.35 p.m. (opposite direction from her apartment).

A large amount of personal information is already collected from the purchases people make with plastic cards. The restricted use made of it at present (it is used mainly to provide bank statements) is because of common-law restrictions on its disclosure which apply to banks, and the expense in processing it. In 1983 the Australian Law Reform Commission's report on privacy predicted strong institutional and commercial interest might eventually encourage the merging of data bases containing personal information and which were outside the restrictions imposed on banks. If this is done, information that has previously been impersonal, in the sense that information about one person was not put together and analysed, will become personalized by the use of systems such as EFTPOS.

An Australian Science and Technology Council report notes that the confidentiality of client information held by banks is becoming less secure. Relationships between banks and other agencies are becoming increasingly complex. Third parties are not bound by the same confidence requirements as banks. Additionally, banks are not bound to keep confidential any information they acquire outside their role of bankers, for example when they are acting as travel agents. In the future, their need to preserve a market share in providing a range of financial services may lead to information exchange practices that are not covered by their traditional obligation to preserve confidence.[7]

EFTPOS terminals will eventually be accessible to a wide range of bank and credit cards so, as more EFTPOS terminals are installed, retailers will increasingly take over some banking functions, such as providing facilities for cash withdrawals, as already mentioned. Partnerships between banks and retailers, such as that proposed by Coles Myer and the Bank of America, mean that retailers would be free, if they wished, to collect and use data gained from the partnership free of the confidentiality restraints imposed on bankers by common law. Such information collection is possible if retailers, rather than banks, own the EFTPOS terminals and operate their own computer network. Information collected in this way could be put to a number of very useful purposes. Retailers could use information collected at the point of sale in aggregate to improve their management and planning. If they were too small to afford the equipment that allows this type of analysis, it is likely that banks would provide these information-processing services for a fee.

The Australian Taxation Office legally collects personal information from magnetic tapes sent to it by Australian banks, to check the amounts of interest declared on tax returns with the bank records. The proposed Australia Card would also form data banks of information about individual actions in opening bank accounts, applying for jobs, selling houses and applying for Commonwealth benefits.

There are legal and commercial justifications for compiling personal profiles from the type of information that could be generated by EFTPOS and by the use of other kinds of computerized information collection. Information collected under an Australia Card number is meant to reduce the amount of tax evasion and social security fraud. Information from banks which is checked by the Australian Taxation Office is also used to reduce tax evasion. However, once EFT-generated information enters the hands of third parties, whether government or private, it can probably only be protected by specific statutory secrecy provisions or by incidental common-law remedies. Even this protection may be inadequate; the Australian Law Reform Commission concludes, in its report on privacy, that when information is disclosed by someone other than the original information provider, the likelihood of error is increased, and it is virtually certain that the information in question will be used for purposes other than that for which it was intended.

One of the fears that people hold is that information will be collected about them without their full knowledge and that it will then be used for purposes of which they are unaware. In 1967 a writer commenting on privacy in the future said that the collection of personal information that was hidden from individuals would gradually bring about the intimacy of an army barracks. He also added that privacy about one's financial affairs, once so entrenched in middle-class values, would become forgotten.[8]

## THE PROS AND CONS OF PRIVACY

Concepts of privacy clearly vary from culture to culture and within society over time. What harm is there in disclosing personal information? The exposure of personal details corresponds to the personal involvement in a relationship. The greater the intimacy between people, the more they are willing to disclose intimate details to each other. To disclose such details to relative strangers may cause changes in individual members of society who in their public opinions tend never to differ from other people. Such unwillingness to be different is often the characteristic behaviour in small societies, and for similar reasons—it is difficult to maintain personal privacy when 'everyone knows everybody else'. Computerized information-gathering may produce, in return for the extra convenience and information useful to reduce crimes and to improve planning, increasingly standardized behaviour on the part of citizens. It also suggests a need for 'habeas data' analogous to the law of habeas corpus which requires that a person may only be held in custody for legitimate reasons., There are at present no similar laws regarding the legitimacy of holding information about individuals. More personal information is often collected than is strictly necessary. It is also used for purposes other than those for which it is collected. Holders of American Express cards are aware of the amount of unsolicited mail which begins to arrive shortly after they have taken out card membership. The Law Reform Commission report notes the sale of lists of people of certain occupations and incomes for direct advertising. The information is gathered from firms or companies who have collected it for other reasons.

Some progress is being made in the protection of personal privacy and this will be discussed later in the chapter.

## MORE COMPUTER USE—LESS REALITY?

Another likely consequence of the widespread use of computers and their ability to collect and process information is that they will change the way in which people think about themselves and about the machines they work with. Sherry Turkle, a sociologist studying children's use of computers, noted that children talked of them as if they were alive, but the criteria they used for defining 'being alive' differed from those used for living creatures. They talked of psychological features they identified in the computers rather than physical characteristics. Turkle believed that this was a positive exercise, in that it encouraged children to raise profound philosophical questions about life and meaning at an early age, and to deal with these questions effectively.[9]

Another anecdote is provided by Joseph Weizenbaum, who wrote a program called Eliza as an experiment to show that artificial intelligence was limited. His program was not intended to encourage users to believe that a computer could really respond in a human way to their questions, but that is what happened. Eliza was built to imitate a conversation between a psycho-analyst and a patient, with the machine taking the role of the analyst. It was programmed to respond to statements with questions or commands. One visitor who tried out the program began the 'session' as follows:

DOCTOR: Good afternoon. Please type in your name. [This was done and the computer continued.] What brought you here to see me today?

VISITOR: Oh, nothing much. I'm feeling a bit tired, that's all.

DOCTOR: Why do you think you're feeling a bit tired?

VISITOR: Well, I've been travelling a lot and away from home.

DOCTOR: Tell me about your family.

To the embarrassment of all present, the visitor settled down to an intimate conversation with the computer without appearing to realize that the program had been set up to caricature what was then a fashionable form of psycho-analysis. Subsequently people were known to contact Weizenbaum to ask for a session with the computer, to 'straighten themselves out'.[10]

Regarding computers as human in some way is perhaps less disturbing than through them losing touch with reality. Discussions with financial counsellors in Australia indicate that the use of ATMs and EFTPOS can distance some people from the use of money to the extent that they become less aware that they are spending too much for their incomes. Once the money management becomes a matter of dealing with machines rather than people, and money itself becomes less tangible, budgeting appears to become more difficult and spending, in some instances, much too easy, thus increasing family debts. This type of detachment means that we run the risk of abrogating personal liability for errors or losses. Banks foresaw this possibility when they increased personal liability for loss of funds in their initial terms and conditions of use for credit cards.

At a much more extreme level, human involvement in wars and attack systems is weakened with the use of expert systems that control battle management, missile attacks and so on. Human involvement in decisions can become limited under these conditions, and the possible destructive effects of people's actions can be blamed on machines rather than on the people who ordered, programmed, installed or monitored them. This detachment is illustrated in an advertisement for systems analysts and programmers. Booz Allen and Hamilton Inc. in, ironically, a hand-written advertisement, ask for strategic defence analysts to deal with SDI policy or architecture issues, computer modelling or simulation or lethality and target-hardening analysis.[11]

There are many advantages in using computers for all kinds of large-scale information processing. In the future they will be used for different functions as intelligent assistants in problem-solving. Their utility then will depend on their advantages to society and to individual outweighing their disadvantages. It would be wrong to blame computers for the latter. They are, after all, the products of human ingenuity and are used as a result of human decisions.

## POLICY IMPLICATIONS

To guide society in a desired direction we need to anticipate the advantages and disadvantages that may occur. Reacting to problems as they arise is a defensive rather than a constructive strategy. Policies that anticipate on the other hand, can increase the ability of society, and the individuals who live in it, to be more in control of the future. This is what we should aim for in making policy.[12] One of the problems Australia may have at the present is that some set of goals for the future are relatively ill-defined. Economic goals are certainly clear, but other social and cultural goals are less specific. In the present environment, the economic goals tend to dominate in the introduction and use of computerized systems. Cost-effectiveness, defined in narrow terms of monetary rather than social and cultural cost, is a major goal.

The issues that have been discussed in this chapter are only some among many. However, they serve to illustrate the complexity introduced into society with the advent of computers. This complexity can be better dealt with if our goals and policies are clearly defined and compatible.

Some of the problems have been recognized and are being addressed. The reduced employment growth which is almost certain in banking and retailing is also a phenomenon in other sectors. These trends appear world-wide in industrialized nations and are being addressed by groups such as the OECD in international discussions. However, the current conclusions are that implementation of any solutions to employment loss will require intense pressure. OECD governments have been asked to address the problem of 'full employment', but in a context that takes into account changes in society as well as changes in technology. Definitions of 'full employment' appear to be changing to an acceptance of a stable 6 per cent to 8 per cent unemployment. Remedies so far include the introduction of a greater variety in hours of work and in continuing training and education. These may be preliminaries to a radical rethinking of what constitutes employment and consideration of the future of work and the distribution of income.[13]

The sheer velocity and volume of information exchange, particularly of financial data, and the possible destabilizing effects on national economies and the international economic order, is an issue that must be taken up by international policy-making bodies.

The privacy of personal information stored in computerized data bases is another question not yet resolved. The introduction of the Australia Card would be accompanied by legislation covering the storage and use of personal information generated by uses of the card. The new legislation would define the use of personal information under guidelines formulated by the OECD and would apply to Commonwealth government departments and to those private-sector organizations which would have to use the number on the card for registering certain transactions. However, there would be inadequate protection of information held in private-sector data bases until at least 1989, when the provisions of the proposed Data Protection Agency might be extended to that sector.

Allied to the question of privacy is the problem of defining the ownership of information held in data bases. Is it the property of the person who gave it, or is it the property of the holder to do with as he or she pleases? Common-law definitions of information and property are being considered while existing law is also confronted with the problem of whether electrical impulses are property (most information transfers take the form of electrical impulses).[14]

Another major policy question is, who is liable when a computer makes errors that cause loss or damage? There is little hesitation in peoples' minds when they are asked that question. Most assume that the owner of the computer is liable: but we have already seen with EFTPOS that it is legally possible to place liability on people other than the owners of the machines. This is an area that requires some further clarification.

Other problems have been less clearly identified, possibly because of the relatively low use of these systems as yet; but major difficulties may lie in the future. This is good reason to anticipate what they may be, and to attempt to defuse them while it is still relatively easy to do so.

There is the little-discussed area of the growing relationship, if that is an appropriate term, between computers and people. There has been some suggestion that programs should be written so that people are always aware that they are dealing with a computer and not with a person; that they can reject the suggestions made by the computer in response to their questions. This is rather counter to the moves to 'user-friendliness' whereby computers are programmed to respond with the user's name as appropriate and to use conventional phrases such as 'please' and 'thank you' when asking users to carry out an operation. The question of how humans and computers can best work together will become more pressing as artificial-intelligence research develops further, particularly as more expert systems and natural language programs are used. We should already be deciding on the best uses for computers. What are humans best at doing and what is the most constructive role for computers?

These questions lie at a different level from national policies over employment, privacy and liability. They may have to be addressed more at the community level, with computer scientists and others working together to resolve the issues. There is at least one group of computer scientists in Australia which is addressing social responsibility issues, but there should be wider debate to assist in their clarification.

A number of commentators believe that computers have become the new 'defining technology' which will change the way in which we think about ourselves and our human identity. Thus the issues are moving from the long-standing concerns over employment, privacy and so on to philosophical questions. Computers and their newer functions, which include artificial intelligence, offer a seduction that may lead us to believe that they will determine technical and social change in the future. It is therefore appropriate to conclude with a reminder that humans and computers have the capacity to work in harmony, and that humans hold the political, economic and social choices that will enable this to happen: 'As our understanding of history increases, it becomes clear that a new device merely opens a door; it does not command one to enter'.[15]

# CHAPTER 7

# WEALTH AND POVERTY IN THE INFORMATION SOCIETY

## Ian Reinecke

A single phrase captures the concerns of many observers about the social and technological trends characterizing what is now commonly described as the information society. It is the expression 'information-rich and -poor'. Behind it is the fear that the social reshaping of which computer and communications technologies are a part will lead to a less just society. Yet while the possibility of greater social division on the basis of access to information is widely canvassed, it remains an imprecise threat. Those who are rich have more cash, property, income and a more luxurious lifestyle than those who are not; but information disparity is a more elusive idea. Just what does it mean?

Barry Jones has outlined the problem in terms of centralized and dispersed control over access to information:

Access to knowledge, capital or wealth is roughly equivalent and there is a widening gap between the information rich and the information poor whereby the unskilled become an intellectual proletariat. The problem of control in an information society is largely unrecognized and undisclosed ... Is access to information to be centralized and subject to monopolist or oligopolist control, or is it to be dispersed, decentralized and widely available?[1]

The problem of control by a minority is familiar, but information introduces a new dimension. How would a society based on information monopoly or oligopoly be structured, and what conditions would create it? Surprisingly few attempts have been made to answer this question, perhaps because the suggested split between information-rich and -poor has such immediate plausibility. But how is information wealth measured?

Unlike dollars, jewels, paintings or other measures of wealth, information wealth does not depend on possession and ownership. Owning a whole library of unread books does not make one richer in information than an assiduous user of a public library's reading room. It is mostly a matter of *what* information one possesses, rather than how much, that is important. Judged by different criteria, information may be irrelevant, useless or even a handicap. There is also the question of time. Information received by one person before everyone else may have much greater value. So factors of access, relevance and timeliness determine the value of information in ways that make it quite different from conventional wealth.

There are other features of information that distinguish it from money. Unlike material goods that are consumed—such as coal by a steelworks—information does not get used up when it changes hands —as it is in bargaining, gossip and in exchange for favours. If I buy a washing machine, the goods themselves pass to me completely; yet information is both transferred and remains where it came from.

It is this kind of complexity that has stampeded most discussion about information wealth and poverty toward the assessment of tangible differences that can be measured by conventional means. Attention is directed to the technologies that deliver information rather than the content itself. The measurement of disparity using technology as the guide has become a more attractive option as more computer and communications systems have been developed. By measuring the distribution of information-handling technology in society, and describing those with the machines as wealthy and those without as poor, a plausible description of the division can be outlined. Such an equation between information wealth and technology begs a number of questions about how the machines are used, by whom and for what; but it has been widely accepted.

Let us look at three broad kinds of information-delivering technologies: those that are oral, those that use print, those that use electronics. There is overlap between the three, but the classifications hold in general.

The primary means by which most information is conveyed in daily life is physiological—the human voice. In conversations, gossip, arguments and chit-chat, information is exchanged on a massive scale. The prevalence of the spoken word poses a problem for those who would measure information wealth by technological currency. No more than vocal cords and a command of language are needed to participate in this form of communication, and both attributes are distributed almost universally throughout the world. The measurement of vocal information flows has focused on the technology by which human voices have been enhanced, preserved and broadcast. The distribution of telephones within societies has become one of the major indicators of information wealth and poverty: the listing of the number of telephones per thousand of population conforms closely to international rankings of standard of living. The patterns of distribution of radio receivers, television sets and recording devices such as cassettes and discs follow suit. Within societies, the affluent upper and middle classes are the first to adopt goods like radios and television sets. As economies of scale reduce prices and as lower incomes rise, the spread of these information-receiving technologies becomes almost universal. Where the economic barriers are highest, such as in the purchase of video cassette recorders, the rate of diffusion is slowest; while some devices have failed to break the barrier between luxury item and mass consumer good—the video telephone of the late 1960s is an example. Here again the superficial equation of information wealth and possession of technology does become questionable when the uses to which the machines are put are considered. Are the heaviest watchers of television the best-informed people? How is one sort of information evaluated against another—pop music radio against Open University television? These are questions that strain the credibility of an approach that assesses information wealth by counting machines.

The technology of printing has undergone great change over the last two decades as electronics have been introduced to it. But the products of that process—which represent technologies themselves—have remained much the same. The familiar ones are books, newspapers and magazines, and by measuring the quantities in which they are produced, some notion of information wealth can be constructed. (Less obvious information-carrying media which are available to almost everyone include public signs and notices, advertising hoardings and labels on cans and packages.) Among countries, it is the developed nations with superior printing and production processes that create the most publications. Within societies, it is the wealthier layers that consume most books, newspapers and magazines. The influence of the advertising market over editorial content—especially in magazines—means in many cases that those who are not affluent are discouraged from buying the publication.

The additional assumed ingredient in equating information wealth with possession of and access to the products of printing technology is literacy. Whereas competence in spoken language is almost universal, despite differences in complexity, not everyone can be assumed to be literate. It is not just that wealthier countries have higher literacy rates; the difference in literacy levels between different sections of even highly developed societies can be vast. That universal literacy cannot be assumed is a point forcefully made by the writer Jonathon Kozol, who has observed: 'Twenty-five million American adults cannot read the poison warnings on a can of pesticide, a letter from their child's teacher, or the front page of a daily paper. An additional 35 million read only at a level which is less than equal to the full survival needs of our society'.[2] So although the USA is undoubtedly regarded as the most information-rich country in the world, its impressive statistics in publishing do not touch a substantial part of its people. These generally hidden variations in literacy within developed countries undermine the equation of technologies for distributing information with wealth and poverty.

The third group of technologies where this assumption is made also requires literacy, but it is the method of delivery rather than what it carries that has attracted attention. Those who confuse a flowering of electronic technology with the creation of an information-rich society exude understandable enthusiasm. Information handling has undergone an extraordinary transformation, especially in the last decade. While mainframe computers are more than a decade old, the much more common micro-computers are just approaching that milestone. The commercial use of data bases, stored on large computers and reached through micro-computers via telecommunications networks, has only developed widely since the late 1970s, as has videotex, which uses computers and telecommunications to bring information to a screen, and teletext, which uses broadcast television signals to do the same thing. And that short list omits digital storing, switching and transmission techniques that have forced a revision of the economics of information handling.

If one machine was selected from this group of technologies for its contribution to expectations of widespread information wealth, it is the micro-computer. Now that the marketing bubble of the early 1980s has burst, predictions of a micro-computer in every home of developed countries have been revised. While cost is one factor that inhibited the rate at which the machines were used at home, it may not have been the most crucial. The very great information-handling capacity of micro-computers exceeded the needs most people had for that technology. Much of the anticipated demand was projected on the basis of what people did in offices. Unlike the telephone, whose adoption was aided by the fact that people had a use for the device— whether it was keeping in touch with relatives, talking to friends or arranging social meetings—micro-computers lacked obvious daily domestic applications.[3] Yet those who do use micro-computers at work, and in some cases at home, have achieved a new ease of access to information. Does that make those who do not use the technology poorer in information?

Those who assess information wealth by taking an inventory of the technology by which it is distributed would clearly answer yes to that question. Any practical tests to determine the issue would founder on the difficulties of isolating technology as the crucial factor in assessing information wealth and poverty. There is a prima facie case that someone denied books, magazines and newspapers would be less well informed than those who possessed them. But books and other publications can be borrowed at little cost from public libraries. Similarly, the 85 per cent of homes in Australia that have a telephone service may house people who on average are better informed than those without. But public telephones are cheap to use and they are widely available. It is only among the group of information-handling technologies that depend on electronics that denial of access has led to a rise in concern about the creation of a class of information-poor.

Suppose government became so alarmed about this technical disparity that it sought to introduce public policies to overcome it. Would the universal availability of electronic information technology eliminate fears of social inequity? If one thing is certain it is that the mechanism by which information technology has been distributed so far—often misleadingly referred to as the free market—favours the already well-off. If the market, encouraged by public policy support of the idea of universal service, took a century and more to put telephones in four out of every five Australian households, how long would diffusion of electronically-based technology take? Some countries have tackled this problem directly, by intervening to create consumer demand for electronic machines that deliver information to the home. The French government's pilot scheme, introducing electronic terminals in public places and in homes to gain access to data bases containing telephone numbers, is one example of this kind of intervention. The strategy has been described as 'nationalizing consumption'.[4]

The French initiative is imaginative in a number of respects. Most importantly, it provides not only the technology to handle information but gives telephone subscribers a reason for using it. In that respect it differs from the simpler expedient adopted by a free-market approach which is to assume that once machines are sold they will find a use. But this has not been the experience of many consumers who bought micro-computers for themselves, only to find that when the first flush of enthusiasm abated there were few uses for the machines. That machines alone will not solve information poverty is obvious on another level. Like books in the hands of people who are illiterate, micro-computers in the possession of those untrained in their use and even fearful of them do not make them information-wealthy. To construct an approach aimed at overcoming information disparity by making electronic technology universally available, public policy would need to go beyond supplying affordable machines.

The sorts of tasks to which micro-computers can be put to reduce information inequity are generally represented in this way: someone at home sits at a terminal, calls up a data base over telephone lines and thereby gains admission to a cornucopia of knowledge. Many otherwise sedate social scientists have attempted to enliven their discussion of the prospects for a society where information is universally available by offering fictional accounts of this phenomenon.[5] As one of them has pointed out, we are witnessing the creation of a new social metaphor. Instead of the sort of centrally controlled and highly developed technological society portrayed by Aldous Huxley in *Brave New World*, a different vision is being created. Wilson Dizard has outlined it in these terms:

We have moved away from these monstrous models towards more humanistic ones, in which machines are subordinate rather than a controlling factor. The cold metaphor of the impersonal, technocratic machine is being replaced. The new metaphor is a blooming, buzzing garden in which each of us—including those new Einsteins and their computers—can cultivate a personal plot.[6]

The trouble with the metaphor is that is ignores the practical realities of using data bases for information retrieval. A micro-computer equipped with a communications board and software can certainly be used to gain access to the large commercial data bases. But it does not solve the problem of how you get the information you want, let alone the information you might need. In many cases, commercial vendors of electronic information protect their data bases by erecting proprietary software around them. Communications costs may represent only a very small proportion of the total subscription to the data base. Software barriers do not end there. Because the major users of data bases are institutions pursuing searches for information delivered in a required format, it is those forms that determine how information is retrieved. Thus while a demographic data base can be used to retrieve mailing lists of affluent consumers, sorted according to postcode, it may be impossible to map neighbourhoods so that housing problems can be highlighted. Any public policy initiative to redress information inequity would have to tackle these difficulties.

Appropriate software is important in another respect. If micro-computers were to be made available to all, the uses to which they can be put—a range restricted by the existence of adequate programs—may render them irrelevant. By far the greatest number of programs sold for micro-computers are those allowing the machines to be used as word processors, or to plan sales and make financial calculations. The paucity of programs that meet potential information needs at home has been blamed as a major factor in the collapse of the home computer boom. Because it is the market that has dictated what software is produced, there are hardly any programs designed for purposes other than satisfying the purposes of corporations, scientific and research bodies, and government agencies and departments. And unlike their use of the telephone, citizens at large are not able to develop uses for the technology off their own bat. Picking up a telephone, dialling a number and talking to the person who answers the call is a process of almost primitive simplicity compared to using a micro-computer to retrieve electronically stored information.

The additional difficulty with the metaphor of information abundance is one that is seldom tackled, partly because of obsessional interest in the technology rather than the messages it carries. If an audit of the information needs of most people as citizens was taken, it would include subjects that are excluded from existing data bases. What interest could the information-poor be expected to take in data bases containing stock market prices, company results, macro-economic statistics, legal precedents, complex medical literature and details about the creditworthiness of companies? The answer is clearly that this is not the sort of information that would be most useful to them. Yet this is the kind of information that dominates commercial activity in the electronic data base industry. There are no commercial data bases specializing in answering information needs such as 'What are my welfare entitlements? Does my landlord have the right to evict me for late rental payments? Is my hire purchase agreement charging excessive interest?'. These are the things that poor people often need to know, but micro-computers and data bases will not provide them.

It might be argued that what to the information-wealthy are very elementary questions about social and legal rights can be answered without recourse to electronic technology. They could be answered by ringing government agencies or reading brochures produced by them. But while both those options have been available for many years, their use has not eliminated information poverty at this basic level. Besides, the metaphor of a blooming, buzzing abundance promises that each of us will have our own plot—and that implies the satisfaction of these sorts of information needs as an absolute minimum requirement.

There are two implications of this deficiency that count against the prospect of electronic technology alone redistributing information wealth more evenly. One is that the technology was never intended to be applied to such mundane tasks. But such a judgement is based on the assumption that these questions are in some sense lower-order requests for information, so basic as to be almost a frivolous use of sophisticated electronic systems. If that is so, the claim that information equity will be improved by the spread of technology depends on a selective view of the world, not to mention justice. The other consequence of a highly technologized society leaving its information-poor untouched is that the power the machines confer on those who can employ them was never intended to be spread very widely. That is, the prospect of becoming information-rich was only ever available to the wealthy, the educated, the middle and upper classes, the articulate and the powerful. If it has been a hidden assumption of much of the fanciful discussion about information abundance that it was not expected to filter down to those with the greatest need, it deserves to be spelled out. In any event, there appears to be an ominous silence on these matters from writers otherwise anxious to extol the benefits of the information society.

Far from leading to a decentralization of information resources, electronic technology is at least as likely to concentrate power as to disperse it. This prediction is based on the pattern in which the technology has already been distributed in the last twenty years. It is to those who have substantial power already that the first use of the technology has gone, for they have shaped its development. By leaving the spread of technology to the market, government bureaucrats, social planners and professional observers of the process have sympathetically presided over the advancement of a class to which they by and large belong. What sort of society might their efforts produce?

The most avid users of electronic information technology belong to the stratum of technically expert people that has preoccupied many thinkers about social change. As Daniel Bell has pointed out, social philosophers such as Saint-Simon had attempted to describe this élite by using the term *technicien*. The immigrant American engineer Thorstein Veblen actually attributed a latent power for radical social change to this class of technologically proficient and information-rich technocrats. And Bell himself estimated the numbers in this class in the late 1960s in the USA at about 300 000, using the National Science Foundation register of scientific and technical personnel as his guide. It was because of their influence that Bell nominated universities as the primary institutions driving society beyond its industrial phase.[7]

Bell's description of these people as 'the engineers of intellectual technology' foresaw their leading role in the introduction of the electronic means of handling information. Their strategic power was such that the techniques they pioneered in computer simulations of economic systems, social behaviour and decision-making theory became essential for public policy-making and corporate strategies.[8] And his vision of the future was influenced by the metaphor of information abundance. He predicted an information utility system in which tens of thousands of terminals would be connected to giant central computers dispensing information on demand.[9] Bell's predictions about the dominance of the technocratic élite were shared in many respects by J. K. Galbraith, although he differed about the institutional focus of power. For Galbraith it was the modern corporation and those who participated in the process by which its decisions were made—he called all those who took part members of the 'technostructure'. These were the planners, the experts, those to whom power passed when specialized knowledge was required.[10]

More colourfully, a critic of both Bell and Galbraith has described the class they identify as 'technical soul brothers acting in the best interests of the corporation'. These are the people 'who have seen the print-out on the wall'.[11] Alvin Toffler, with a journalistic flair for a single word to express the idea, labelled these people 'the cognitariat', to distinguish them from the proletariat of an industrial age. What is more, as a class it would have greater political power than the proletariat it displaced, using knowledge rather than muscle to earn rewards and effect social change.[12] In any description of a society which was stratified into layers that were progressively wealthier in information, the cognitariat would be at the top. It is at least possible that those who are at the top will turn out to be benign, humanitarian, progressive and committed to social justice; but there is a wealth of human experience to suggest that without stringent accountability such a class will be tempted to wield power for its own advantage. What is most under threat in such societies is the capacity of democratic structures to restrain excessive pursuit of self-interest.

If power over technology and knowledge is not to be ceded to the cognitariat, some process of public policy planning is required; choices ought not to be made in advance for people about the society they would prefer to live in. Preserving a possibility of choice requires initiatives that regulate the expansion of influence of those who are already powerful. What measures could be adopted to ensure that this problem of control is recognized? How can we ensure that information is not centralized, that it is dispersed and widely available? Both these questions were asked some time ago by Barry Jones. In outlining a policy and legislative programme that would in his words show 'the way out of the flybottle', he proclaimed: 'Monopolist or oligopolist control of information is as unthinkable as entrepreneurial control of air, water or sunlight for profit'.[13] In an earlier aside Jones declared that if the issue was not publicly discussed in Orwell's year of 1984 'it may mean that the battle for control has—unnoticed—already been won by oligopolists and centralizers'.[14]

What public discussion there has been of information inequity has barely ruffled the surface. In one sense that is understandable, for measures which promote the development of a fairer society in general do advance the goal of information equity. But few specific proposals directed at redistributing information wealth have been given a public airing. Indeed, there have been proposals in the opposite direction, such as calls for the government to hand Telecom Australia to private investors. I have argued elsewhere that such a move has a direct impact on the information-poor, in many cases making them worse off than before.[15] Precious little attention has been paid to how we might change the *status quo* to attack the causes of information poverty. It is a task that requires a clear understanding of what information people need, as opposed to what information-wealthy institutions are prepared to pay for, as well as widespread opportunities to acquire ease in handling information technology. For once the skills to seek specific information are developed in society at large, they can be directed at redressing the balance of information power, using technology that is appropriate to the task.

One group of the information-rich for whom inequity is a continuing concern is the library community. Unfortunately, their debates have seldom moved into general circulation. The special role of libraries is recognized in the national information policy adopted at the Federal conference of the ALP in 1982, which gave this expression to the demand for equity: 'All Australians are entitled to free access to information and library services of acceptable standard, regardless of where they live, of their social and economic position, language, sex, age, mobility or physical disabilities'. And on the plight of the information-poor it declared: 'Information facilities are remote from those who need them most. They do not know what is available and do not know how to remedy their lack of information'. This policy has been one of the least discussed questions of social justice in Australia, although debate has been more vibrant in other countries.

In the USA the National Commission on Libraries and Information Science (NCLIS), adopted these goals ten years ago: 'To eventually provide every individual in the United States with equal opportunity of access to that part of the total information resource which would satisfy the individual's educational, working, cultural and leisure-time needs and interests, regardless of the individual's location, social or physical condition or level of achievement'. The implementation of such aims depends very much on the political complexion of the administration in power, and optimism about their being put into practice waned after 1980.

Attempts to define information poverty absorbed a White House conference on library and information services in 1979, where these points were made in its discussion guide on meeting personal needs.

The number of books in print has risen more than 25 per cent in the past five years. This is just a partial indication of the tremendous growth in information production and consumption. And the growth is not only in the area of scientific information but in the type and amount of 'life-information'—information an individual needs to successfully negotiate his or her way through life.

As our society moves further away from the nuclear family, as social structures change, and as we become more geographically mobile, traditional life-information systems such as friends and family are less accessible.

Equal access to information is a natural extension of democratic principles. If information is a public good and an informed individual contributes to the benefit of society as a whole, then access to information must be guaranteed—not only in principle but in fact.

. . . information is needed more by the educationally and economically deprived because they have not had the opportunity to acquire information that others have had. There are needs for special packaging and provision of information for the unserved. The poor often have limited energy and resources to spend on information because of the daily struggle to survive.[16]

But it is just those people who are least touched by the transformation of the technological means of handling information more efficiently. And the conceptually simple expedient of transferring the technology, the software and the data bases of the information-rich down to the poor will not solve their problems of deprivation. Not only is the technology intimidatory, the software inappropriate and the information in the form it is offered in data bases irrelevant, but the cost is prohibitive. All four factors need to be tackled in any approach that hopes to improve the plight of the information-poor.

Why has so little attention been paid if the urgent need to prevent a widening rift between information-rich and -poor has been recognized, although not widely debated? The complexity and scale of information disparity is one answer. Widespread preoccupation with the most recent products of the manufacturers of electronic information handling systems is another. But it may also be the general reluctance to concede that the market and its technological offerings are responsible for widening the gap. This technological blind faith is not confined to the field of computers and communications. Those who have tried to raise alternatives to hydro-electric and nuclear power generation have had difficulty in being taken seriously in mainstream discussion. Much of the hostility they attract appears to stem from the fear that serious consideration of their ideas would be a stepping back from progress, a vote of no confidence in technology-driven solutions to human needs.

Yet specific projects that embody the principles of relevance, cost and efficiency have been devised, albeit with little support from the institutions that dominate the technological provision of information. I will outline just one, not as a model for answering all the information needs of the information-poor but as a beginning. Its starting point is that most people whom we would expect to be information-poor rely very much more on oracy than literacy in finding out what they want to know. That may be because English is not their first language, or because they were obliged to leave school early, or because the schools they went to did not have the staff and resources to ensure higher levels of literacy among all their students. But it may also be because oral traditions in their families, their communities and in their work-places are stronger than in the lives of the information-rich. An academic, for instance, would rely more heavily on literacy for information than most builder's labourers, bus drivers and shop assistants. To make that point implies no judgement about the relative worth of the information to the individual concerned.

Oral exchanges are, however, excluded from almost all the information systems devised to run offices, production lines, battleships and aircraft. The exceptions, in the form of computer simulations of human speech, are still peripheral in even the most recent information systems. Because of factors such as mobility and changing social attitudes, many oral information networks in neighbourhoods and among family and friends have fractured. Contact by voice increasingly requires technological assistance and the telephone has provided it. On a more formal basis, the spread of information hotlines, emergency telephone advice services and specialist switchboards for women, gay people and victims of rape or child sexual abuse demonstrate the effectiveness of oral communication. To encourage such operations is not to discard literacy but to recognize that the preoccupation of the information-rich with the printed—or screen-displayed—word blinds them to the realities of information poverty.

If librarians are, as some of them term themselves, information scientists, practising a science of the printed word, there may be other workers who have a similar facility with oral communication. Many people need to be skilled communicators in their work—in selling, providing advice, teaching, public speaking and dealing with inquiries—but one group combines both facility with the spoken word and the technological means of delivering it. Telephone operators, the traditional information switches of rural Australian communities when all exchanges were manual, combined those qualities. In recent years they have added the operation of data bases to their skills, as computerized directory inquiry systems have been introduced. They provide a ready-made workforce to translate the information needs of the information-poor into the facts and figures that will assist them.

Because computers are such efficient machines for ordering information, matching relevant details and rapidly retrieving data, they have a function in a project using oral delivery of messages. By providing telephone operators with electronic technology and devising software that will quickly provide information in the format required by callers, queries can be efficiently answered. As for the information these data bases should contain, much of it exists in the community already: in citizen's advice bureaus, legal aid centres, libraries, local government services, welfare and volunteer organizations, clubs and societies. By enabling those information sources to store their information on the computer systems used by telephone operators to display it, there are reciprocal advantages.[17] Callers have access to 'life-information'. Community groups and government agencies have a record of their information that can be updated from a micro-computer, printed out, or typeset. And telephone operators, threatened with the elimination of their skills, are given fruitful employment with expanded responsibility and greater job satisfaction.

No matter how well such schemes work, it might be argued, they do not tackle head-on the problems of information control in society. By devising such projects to run in parallel with the technologically more complex information-handling systems of large institutions, energy might be diverted away from the central problem of control. But once the main barrier to wider discussion of the general issues of information control is identified, the role of such projects becomes clearer. The first step is to convince people that these questions matter. How does one bring them to the attention of governments, corporations, trade unions and the community? Dramatizing the problem through trials such as the one outlined is one way of giving a human dimension to what otherwise appears a remote issue. Local projects that involve many sections of the community serve to raise the issues at a number of levels, not just confine the debate to the ranks of the information-rich. Moreover, the practical task of defining information needs that are not met by other methods gives the problem a human scale.

If one were to pose the question 'What sort of society do you want to live in, one where information is centralized or one where it is democratized?' most people would opt for latter. But the secondary questions are much more difficult. Is information in our society now under too tight a control? How is disparity to be identified and remedied? The big social choices people make are made up of a series of options with which they are presented almost daily. For most people, the option of living in a society where information justice is assured has barely been visible. As with many other issues of social justice, seeing that there is a problem is the most important breakthrough.

# CHAPTER 8

# LIBRARY RESOURCES IN THE AGE OF INFORMATION TECHNOLOGY

## Averill Edwards

The effect of information technology on libraries has been profound. At first seen as a means of improving scientific and technical reference services, information technology has transformed virtually all aspects of libraries and library activities. Acquisition, cataloguing, reference services and inter-library loans have all been changed. The physical layout of libraries and their buildings, and the collections themselves, have likewise been affected. The widespread introduction and use of computers into libraries has coincided with a political climate conducive to reductions in resources for libraries—both of staff and money. The use of automation has allowed libraries to compensate to some degree for this decline in resources, especially in staff.

This chapter canvasses the notion of an information explosion, its effect and policy implications on libraries, their services and resources. The impact of information technology on the traditional cataloguing areas of collection development, on resource sharing, staff, training and the physical environment in libraries is explored. New problems for libraries have been created by the introduction of information technology—new forms of material, enormous increases in quantity, the need for preservation, confidentiality, standards, occupational health and safety, and the cost of the new services—problems which pose a challenge to the continuing existence of libraries.

The importance of the entrepreneurial role of librarians must be recognized. Increasingly, librarians are being drawn outside their four walls, as evidenced by their active participation in the development of a national information policy. Changes in libraries, their resources and activities will require changes to access and service policies. Libraries will have to package and sell information. The effects may be so profound that we may be looking at widespread de-institutionalization of libraries.

## A NEW LOOK FOR LIBRARIES

The development of a central on-line data base at the Ohio College Library Centre in 1971 showed for the first time the cost saving which could come from having a book catalogued only once for a group of libraries, with all others accessing that record on the central automated data base. Many other networks, both small and large, have followed this example. In Australia, in 1981 the National Library established the Australian Bibliographic Network (ABN) to be the first nation-wide on-line data base, to which libraries throughout Australia could have access and contribute cataloguing data. Reduction in unit costs for cataloguing books and serials, savings in staff costs, wider and faster availability of information, and better use of collections have resulted from the establishment of ABN. Other regionally based cataloguing networks exist in Australia, but ABN with five million records is the largest. Cataloguing from the Library of Congress, the British Library, the national libraries of Canada and New Zealand is sent to the National Library regularly and mounted on the data base. Participants within Australia contribute original cataloguing also. In August 1986 there were 121 libraries as participants—that is they can catalogue their books on line—while 380 other libraries can access the data base by dial-up facilities, and this number is increasing. The adoption by the National Library of New Zealand and by the National Library of Singapore of the same software as ABN has raised the prospect of a wider regional network, and the same software has just been chosen by the National Library of China for use in its national system.

Originally ABN listed only books, serials and newspapers. Since 1984 the National Library of Australia (NLA) has explored with pilot projects entry of other forms of material—music, maps, manuscripts and pictorial items. In 1986 a complete listing of the oil paintings held in the NLA collection was put into ABN, using international cataloguing standards for the description of the material. The availability of such information on line to other Australian libraries has resulted in an increase in inquiries and in the use of the collection. It is clear that other types of material will be added not only to ABN but to other similar networks in the future, resulting in more effective access to the nation's library collections and a better service for patrons.

The 1980s have seen in Australia the development of turnkey systems for automation of purchase of library materials. The development of integrated systems for acquisition, cataloguing and circulation has produced more efficient services, cheaper and faster than manual systems. A typical issue of *InCite*, the fortnightly newsletter of the Library Association of Australia (LAA), has advertisements for six automated systems for libraries.

Academic and public libraries have for many years used automated circulation systems to control borrowings: these systems are now being integrated with other automated systems in use in libraries. The NLA is examining the possibility of mounting an inter-library loan system on ABN which would enable libraries to locate a document anywhere in Australia and then by use of electronic mail facilities request a loan of that item from the holding library, resulting in a faster service for users.

Reference services have been transformed by the use of information technology. Long searches too tedious for manual search are now possible. Document delivery of the items can be requested by telex or electronic mail and despatch effected by facsimile. Access to overseas data bases has been made possible by the use of satellite technology. For a geographically isolated country such as Australia it is important that access to overseas literature, as well as to Australian literature, should be available, but it raises questions of Australian dependence on overseas information, and means that libraries have a vital interest in national and international communications policies.

Facsimile transmission of documents is not new; however, recent technological improvements have made facsimile so much faster that it now has some real possibility for use in inter-library loans. A directory being compiled in the NLA lists some eighty libraries with access to facsimile transmission in Australia. The development of machines which both photocopy and then transmit pages from a bound item will eliminate one of the difficulties for libraries in the use of facsimile machines, although for it to be used extensively, even faster transmission will be needed than forty seconds per page. For urgent requests it has ended the dependence on physical transmission of the loan items via post or courier services.

One of the effects of the use of information technology in libraries has been the de-institutionalization of librarianship. In the past, it was necessary to go to such a physical storehouse of books and serials, serviced by librarians, to find information. It is now possible to establish an information service outside a library and provide a perfectly adequate service. Searching of data bases requires a terminal and communication lines to data bases or data-base vendors/ networks, and these can be provided from a home or an office building. Companies can now offer an information service with 24-hour access to data bases. The move out into the community has made librarians more visible and made their particular skills more evident. It has also required librarians to develop new entrepreneurial skills. Provision of the actual documents identified still requires access to a physical storehouse—but for how long? It is possible now to access the full text of certain articles in the *Bulletin* via Ausinet,[1] the ACI Computer Services public data-base network, and the full text of other Australian overseas journals and reference texts are available to searchers. The movement of librarians into private enterprise and outside institutions has resulted in a change of name—now they are known as 'information officers' or variants on that theme, but not 'librarians'. Often these people take on other information tasks— organization of file registries, company information, etc., within those bodies.

The Victorian State government has developed in the 1980s a category of 'information manager' as part of an institutionalized career structure for librarians, archivists, information officers and computer systems officers.[2] Each category has its own career structure but each leads to the post of 'information manager'. In developing this category the Victorian Public Service Board was seeking to establish common work-value standards and common levels of skill and knowledge. These persons have responsibility for the provision of a broad spectrum of information services in departments. Increasingly an integrated approach is made to information provision within departments, with libraries as only one of several sources.

With the introduction of information technology, there has been a shift of professional staff from cataloguing areas into the reference areas, where more assistance is offered to readers. New areas of activity have been introduced into libraries—computer professionals are part of the staff structure of major libraries, now that more library operations are automated. Allen B. Veanor predicts four changes in staffing patterns:

• fewer cataloguers, none in smaller libraries, because of the use of centralized automated data bases;
• fewer clerks, as routine clerical operations are provided by turnkey systems;
• fewer staff working on inter-library loans, as commercial document delivery systems are used;
• shift of librarians to computing areas to work on information systems design.[3]

Physical planning within buildings is now easier. In the past, the card catalogue had to be physically accessible to staff and users. With on-line catalogues, physical proximity to the one catalogue is not required—all that is needed is a terminal giving access to the central data base.

Libraries have ceased being merely storehouses of information. Whilst they will not lose that function, libraries must develop into *active* centres of information. Many other groups are competing with libraries now in the provision of information—private firms, co-operative networks, government departments and authorities, individuals. These are all able to compete with libraries in providing information, because of the new information technology. If libraries are to retain their place as centres of excellence and expertise, they are going to have to be much more entrepreneurial, with much more of their resources spent on promotional activities. The use of a private firm by a researcher will cost money; the service offered by a library may be offered free but it may take too long. Cost-effective services tailored to specific needs will have to be developed by libraries or else they will be outdone by other bodies eager, willing and able to do so.

Accountability and effectiveness are the new catch-cries for libraries—increased accountability to their governing and funding authorities. Information technology will help libraries in this task, but services will have to be more forcefully and effectively marketed. Ian McCallum isolated some of the characteristics of the Australian population taken from the Australian Bureau of Statistics Social Indicators and urged libraries to adapt their services to a changing clientele.[4] A recent survey of youth referred to the fact that many rarely enter libraries, read only a few magazines and some newspapers but watch TV, films and videos and listen to radio, tapes and records. McCallum urged libraries to examine their services in the light of this information. Promotion of their activities and services in newspapers and in libraries will reach few—eye-catching notices in pubs and supermarkets would be more effective, as would use of radio and videos. It is of paramount importance for libraries to be adaptable, flexible and responsive, to make future services meet the needs of the clientele: if they do not, they will wither. Libraries will need to undertake market surveys to identify their users more closely, to isolate the precise markets for their products and services and to develop appropriate and needed services and abandon outmoded and unused services. Innovation and imagination allied to the expanding capacity of the new technology will be essential. Information technology offers the opportunity for libraries to provide information in a variety of formats and in a variety of packages: it must not be lost.

The development of new forms of information is changing the dimensions of libraries and their services. Researchers in the humanities have long thought that there was little benefit to them from automation. Professor Ching-Chih Chen of Simmons College, Boston, stated that with the development of compact-disc read-only memory storage (CD-ROM), the capacity to store an image had finally brought specific benefits to the humanities.[5] The bibliographic citation of a picture can now be accompanied by an excellent three-dimensional image and can be offered remote from the collection. The NLA and the Library of NSW are exploring the possibility of storing on video-disc the pictorial treasures of both their collections. Such a disc could then be made available to researchers throughout Australia, enabling more thorough research and less expensive travel prior to a visit. The usefulness of CD-ROM will extend to on-line data bases. Large-scale bases or portions of them could be placed on compact disc and distributed to libraries in regional areas. The data base on disc plus software and appropriate hardware could form a package to be used to develop a regional data base of holdings for use by local libraries. The enormous compaction of information on CD-ROM will mean more efficient storage for libraries with large computing installations.

Printed books and serials will remain with libraries for the foreseeable future because they are convenient and easy to use, but such collections are increasingly being supplemented by information in other forms. Video collections are common and films, sound recordings and tapes are widely used. The NLA recently administered a Community Employment Program project on the cultural context of unemployment, which used as its information base tapes of interviews with different categories of unemployed people in Australia, these tapes to be placed in the Library for the use of researchers in the future. Eric Wainwright suggests that two parallel systems of access to information will be maintained by libraries in future—one for electronic and one for print formats.[6]

Microfilm will continue to transform storage and preservation in libraries, allowing compact storage of many pages of information as well as offering the means to conserve rare items. The National Library in 1984–85 had 1.6 million volumes in microform.[7] In 1984 university libraries in Australia had over two million volumes in microform.[8]

All major libraries in Australia are linked by telex, but that network is being supplemented by the electronic mail network. Many private and public suppliers of electronic mail systems have appeared in the market and are serving the specific needs of libraries; wider adoption of such technology will increase communication and contact between libraries across Australia. With the announcement by the NLA of its support for the Overseas Telecommunications Commission's Minerva system, it is likely that libraries will concentrate on that system.

Libraries are using videotex to provide up-to-date information. Public libraries in Victoria have agreed to provide in their branches access to Viatel, a videotex system launched by Telecom. Major applications include electronic mail, telephone directory and health information services.

The adoption of automation and information technology in libraries has had an effect on training for librarianship. For many years now, courses in basic computing and systems development have been included in training courses at tertiary institutions for professional librarians, and bridging courses have been provided for those untrained in automation. Training in the use of information technology has been undertaken by library technicians and by clerical staff who work in libraries. In the future, few workers in libraries will not be conversant with information technology of some sort and use it in their daily work. New criteria are needed for staff selection—training in and familiarity with computers are sought. The days of libraries as a retreat from the world by the introverted are long gone. Veanor addresses at some length the new requirements for librarians. Amongst those competencies he identifies are management ability, flexibility and adaptability, entrepreneurial attitudes, scientific detachment, intellectual skills and commitment to librarianship, financial management skills, mechanical skills and leadership. It is 'a profession that is deeply intellectual and highly technical, not an employment opportunity for those who "love books" or "enjoy reading" nor a "game room" for those who enjoy "playing" with computers'.[9] Outgoing, innovative staff are needed at all levels. Emphasis on training courses showing how to use information technology, on analysis and planning will be needed if librarians are to cope with the challenge of the future. It is essential that such skills are developed during training, so that newly graduated staff do not start in their first job unfamiliar with a terminal and the basic workings of a system or ill-equipped for a career of constant change. Any cataloguer working in Australia needs to be familiar with ABN and to have had training time on the system, and library schools must be funded adequately so that such appropriate training can be provided.

The major professional association for librarians in Australia is the Library Association of Australia. Its objects are to promote and improve libraries and library services and to improve the standard of librarianship and the status of the profession. In 1984 the General Council of the LAA established a Corporate Plan and Review Committee (CPRC). The terms of reference for the Committee included preparation of a corporate plan for the LAA, a review of existing structure and functions and recommendations for alternative structures and functions to better meet the objectives of the Association.[10]

In a series of hearings held throughout Australia, it was clear that amongst several main issues a change of name was considered necessary by many members. Libraries and librarians are and will be involved in information in the wider use of that term. Librarians are working in information services: there are workers in information areas who are not librarians but to whom the LAA and its activities are relevant. The present name was considered by many to place too narrow a framework for the Association to develop in the future. The LAA would not wish to, and it cannot, represent all information workers in this country, but there are significant numbers which it can support. To survive the LAA must broaden its scope and objectives to match the expansion of the role of libraries, and reflect that scope in a new name. In June 1985 General Council agreed to a new name, Library and Information Association of Australia (LIAA) and supported a change in functions to reflect the wider involvement of libraries and librarians beyond the confines of institutions. The CPRC recommended that new services be introduced to members, concentrating on the information manager and the new technology and widening eligibility criteria for professional membership.

With the current changes taking place in the information industry there is also a cross disciplinary shake-up occurring. This shake-up will continue for the next 5–10 years but the Association must take action now to ensure that it is attracting its share of the information profession. This does not mean ignoring the needs of library personnel but the plain fact is that the role and nature of traditional library work has undergone enormous change. As well as this there are increasing numbers of librarians moving into other than traditional library jobs. The Association must cater for all these needs and is in a good position to do so.[11]

Unless the LAA makes genuine efforts to implement the recommendations of the CPRC to meet the changes in librarianship, it will contract into a small and insignificant grouping representing traditional print-oriented librarians.

The increasing emphasis on cost recovery and accountability by government and institutions has resulted in considerable pressures on libraries to charge for services. Traditionally inter-library loans have been exchanged free of charge between libraries. In a country such as Australia, with vast distances and scarce resources, inter-library loan has always been heavily used. The availability of on-line data bases has made it easier to locate documents. Increasing use of the inter-library loan system as a result of holdings listed in on-line bibliographic systems and reductions in purchasing by libraries has placed great pressures on libraries with large collections. Estimates of costs for individual transactions range from $8 to $25. In 1981 charges were introduced for supply of photocopies of journal articles as required by the *Copyright Act*: current cost (1987) is $3 per article. Traditionally no change has been made for the loan of books. In June 1986 one university library announced that in certain situations a charge of $15 would be made for an inter-library loan, whether for a photocopy or for a book.

Charges for services challenge a long-held philosophy by libraries—that such services should be supplied free of charge. Can libraries continue to support the high cost of inter-library loans? Will information technology provide a solution—full text on optical disc which can then be transmitted electronically to the requesting library? The Library of Congress has an optical disc pilot project, to convert the text of serials onto video disc as they are acquired by the Library. The four-year project is designed to evaluate the use of the new technology for information preservation, storage, retrieval and costing in a library environment. Copyright problems notwithstanding, the technology is there to solve the problem of inter-library loans in the long term. The problem of charging will still be there—but will it be so pressing?

Libraries are facing a new kind of user. The widespread use of computing facilities in educational institutions means that more users are computer-literate—they are familiar with computer terminals and are willing to use a variety of media to gain information. Libraries have to adapt to the demand of these new users. On-line public access catalogues (OPAC) are 'user-friendly' catalogues designed to be easy to use and to be located in public areas. CAVAL, a consortium of Victorian academic libraries and the National Library, is to test Cool-cat, a user-friendly, comprehensible and accessible on-line system for access to information about location of books in six Australian libraries. It is one of several such systems proposed for use in Australian libraries.

Libraries have also to be aware of the group of users who are not familiar with computers—the older users, the less privileged—and services to provide them with appropriate access to information will need to be developed.

## NEW PROBLEMS FOR LIBRARIES: THE INFORMATION EXPLOSION

The phrase 'information explosion' is a well-worn one but describes succinctly a phenomenon which has had a significant effect on libraries. Statistics are hard to come by and confusing, but it is generally agreed that an enormous increase in publishing of information in many forms has been one of the main characteristics of the twentieth century and for libraries one of its most challenging features. The United Nations *Statistical Year Book* over the years has provided statistics on the number of books published world-wide.[12] Librarians are aware of the number of new books and journals published each year. No library would ever be able (or want) to keep them all, although it is more difficult to select items for the collection from the bewildering array available. But there is not only an explosion of printed materials: more data bases are being created each year and even information technology is not able to cope adequately with control or access to it. The growth has no foreseeable end—continual improvements in information technology enable more and more information to be stored and to be accessed easily.

The increase in information has coincided with a period of restraints on funding: thus information technology has enabled libraries to cope with demand. The size and pattern of population in Australia, the great distances, combined with a small population and scarcity of resources for libraries, have led to the development of greater inter-dependence between Australian libraries and contributed to the development of much co-operative activity. The national inter-library loan system, the development of CAVAL, CLANN and ABN as co-operative cataloguing networks has been made possible by use of information technology. Co-operation has extended informally to recognition of existing specific collection strengths as a guide in collection development. The devaluation of the Australian dollar will mean that less information can be acquired by Australia, either as books or in access to overseas data bases. Warren Horton, Director-General of the National Library, has called for greater rationalization and co-ordination of library resources. Mr Horton has proposed what he described as a 'once in a generation strategic planning exercise' by the nation's libraries to identify the difficulties and opportunities confronting libraries. The end result of a series of regional and then national discussions would be 'the landmark occasion on which the profession takes the next great leap forward in developing co-operative service to the nation'.[13] Great interest has been shown in this proposal and initial planning has begun.

The availability of five million records on ABN, many with Australian locations, provides the opportunity for libraries to undertake some Australia-wide rationalization of collections. Warren Horton has suggested that with this information widely available on line, now is the time for more formal agreements to be reached between libraries on which one will collect what. Such a proposal will not be easy to achieve but is not impossible. If libraries are to cope with the challenges of control of and access to available information by 2000 AD then some such approach must be adopted. Michael Gorman describes co-operation as 'not an activity libraries may or may not choose to engage in—it is the element in which they live and prosper. Co-operation is as essential to a library as is water to a fish or air to a mammal'. He goes on to stress a view in which all libraries are part of the totality of library service. He describes what he calls 'The Library', a mega-network made up of co-operative endeavours of many kinds and sizes to which all library users will have access. Electronic bibliographic control systems are the technological tool which will enable institutions to achieve the new co-operation. His library of the future is described as a 'web of hitherto undreamed of resources created by co-operation and the intelligent and creative use of technology'.[14]

The increase in the creation and availability of data bases and the accelerated growth in the information industry in Australia was a factor in the creation of the Australian Database Development Association in 1982. Representing public- and private-sector bodies, data-base producers and on-line services, ADDA's objectives are primarily to provide a focus for communication with users of Australian data bases, government and other appropriate bodies, to formulate policies on the development of Australian data bases and to exchange information. ADDA hopes to have some influence on issues related to the development of and access to public Australian data bases: and it has become an active organization.

Libraries are now having to face competition from other services: and users are willing to pay a fee for this service. Libraries have to face the dilemma of breaking with their tradition of 'free' (to the user) services or charging for access to information. Patricia Battin says

the emergence of an information industry which views information as a commodity rather than a public good is causing an alarming shift in the perception of value from the intellectual quality of information to a value based on short-term market demand.[15]

Information technology has provided quick and easy access to a variety of data bases, but at a cost—easily identifiable costs. It is easy for administrators to urge charging for use of these sophisticated services. To what extent should libraries continue to absorb these high access and communications costs? Should they be passed on to the end user? Frequently the end user is able to pay and has access to corporate finance or research grants to do so. What problems will be experienced by users if fees are charged? How many will be disadvantaged by not having the money to pay a fee for a service? How are users to find the $20 for an ERIC search to provide an article on the practical means to overcome the dyslexia of their child? Are these users to go without, or to rely on less efficient, slower and less effective manual services? What will it mean for our society as a whole, where survival depends so much on possession of information, if it is divided into 'the information-rich' and 'the information-poor'—those who can pay and those who cannot?

Libraries have faced this dilemma for some time but have not solved it. The LAA in 1979 adopted a formal policy statement on charging for services which stresses the right of all Australians to obtain information and resolutely opposes charging fees for access to information, whether it is provided by information technology or not. 'Freedom of access to published information is essential to the democratic process and to the social welfare of the community. That freedom can be inhibited as much by poverty as by censorship. Satisfaction of a person's information needs must not be contingent upon his ability to pay'.[16] This is a strong statement, yet it is a fact that many libraries in the country charge for on-line services.

It can be argued that in times of greater accountability more expensive services should be a charge on the user, but the basic difficulty still exists—what do you provide for those who need information and cannot pay? Libraries have to resolve this problem if they are to continue to be a free source of information to this democratic community and not become a fee-for-service institution. Ian Reinecke outlines the situation in the USA, describing the respective stands taken by the Information Industry Association and the American Library Association. Reinecke warns that there are poor grounds for thinking that Australia will not face a similar conflict over charging for use of electronic information systems, and if the view of what is humane is to prevail, then librarians, to preserve free access, will need to fight hard to see that adequate allocation of resources to libraries is made to enable them to do so.[17]

The increased use of electronic storage of data has created another problem for libraries—preservation of electronic data. Libraries have been able to preserve data in the past to show the state and extent of information in a particular area at a particular time. With on-line systems data are constantly changed to keep them up to date and unless a specific attempt is made to preserve them at a particular point, no historical record will be available. In electronic compilation of cartographic information the problem is particularly evident. Some maps only exist in digital form; how should these be preserved? The state of the ABN data base can be determined at fixed points in time by examination of a microfiche copy of the entire data base. As the data base grows, it may become uneconomic to keep it, even on microfiche. The capture and preservation of data has long been a library prerogative; information technology has made it possible for this role to disappear and with it the preservation of society's records for future research.

The use of information technology has raised questions of privacy and confidentiality of records. Records of who borrows what have always been confidential in libraries. The use of electronic circulation control systems means that better records can be kept and accessed. The same can be said for electronic searches which are undertaken for users. Special steps must be taken to preserve such records from illegal access or use. Under the Copyright Act libraries are now required to keep copies of all photocopy requests, such items to be available to the representatives of copyright owners to enable them to verify that the copying provisions of the Act are not being violated. These records must be protected from unauthorized use.

All libraries supply many photocopies from their printed resources, and it is anticipated that electronic despatch by facsimile will increase such demands. On the other hand, a major revision of the Copyright Act in 1968 defined very specific limits for copying by libraries. The demands by users for access to information held in libraries versus the rights of the copyright owners (authors or publishers) are in conflict, a conflict exacerbated by the ease with which copies can be made. The present Act represents an uneasy balance between the demands of users, libraries, educational institutions, and those of publishers and authors. The government has had the problem of unauthorized electronic copying of audio-visual material under consideration since 1980 and appears no closer to resolution. In parliament recently Senator Durack 'registered our disappointment and criticism that the Government has not tackled the problem of audio-visual copying on a much greater scale than it has in the Bill'. Senator Puplick in the same debate stated that the rate of advances in technology makes it almost impossible for the law to keep pace: 'I believe that the increase in technology and the pace of technology means that the traditional way in which we have understood copyright and the whole framework of intellectual property legislation in this country is doomed'.[18] The problems posed by the Copyright Act and the ease of electronic copying of materials in libraries remains to be solved in a fashion which recognizes the rapid development of electronic technology, the needs of users *and* the rights of copyright owners—not an easy task.

The introduction of information technology has allowed the development of networks at national, State and local levels in libraries. Whilst these are beneficial to those in the network, it is clear that even greater benefit would result from linkage of each network to the other. Protocols and standards within each network vary, and it would be a denial of the potential of information technology to not have networks easily able to connect. The National Library of Canada has for five years been developing a standard communications protocol, Open Systems Interconnection (OSI), for use between different networks, which it is hoped will be adopted in North America. This would allow a national network in which a number of systems and networks could exchange data without the need for multiple systems. The advantages are clear but there is much work to be accomplished before systems can interconnect easily. Not only would libraries need to adopt OSI but major electronic mail system providers and vendors of turnkey systems in Australia would have to agree to develop OSI interfaces. The National Library in July 1986 established a working group on library interconnections with membership to include major library networks and commercial vendors. Its terms of reference include the drafting of OSI standards for Australia, sharing of information about such standards and encouragement of their use. It is hoped that this group will find a practical means to allow national, local and regional library systems to interconnect with each other by means of a standard protocol. Major deterrents to wider introduction are likely to be conflicting political or commercial interests.

As have other organizations introducing information technology, libraries have had to deal with problems of occupational health and safety. Some clerical jobs in libraries have radically changed from on-the-feet jobs to static, terminal-tied jobs. Appropriate courses training staff to use these systems and cope with dislodgement and the fear of electronic technology have had to be developed. Rapidly increasing levels of repetitive strain injury (RSI) amongst professional and clerical staff have forced libraries to create more appropriate and comfortable environments, to design and introduce ergonomically designed chairs and tables, to redesign jobs, to restructure work practices to ensure no person is at a terminal full-time. The ease and speed of information technology was an unfortunate encouragement to the conscientious worker to improve work performance to intolerable levels, with consequent physical damage. Eye strain and residual radiation from terminals have been concomitant problems. In the past, librarians' concern with occupational health hardly extended beyond concern at lifting heavy volumes or dust inhalation. As more technology is introduced into libraries, great care has to be taken to establish it in a positive way and into an appropriate physical environment. Additional training demands arise, as well as industrial problems with conflicts between job classifications and structures, as information technology is introduced.

## NATIONAL INFORMATION POLICY AND LIBRARIES

The first interest in the National Information Policy (NIP) in Australia began in the 1960s and was enunciated in the STISEC Report, the report of the Scientific and Technological Information Services Enquiry Committee, published in May 1973. The report commented on the lack of a national information policy in Australia and, in particular, of a science and technology information policy. It concluded that urgent and growing needs could only be met by co-ordinating and assisting existing library and information services, and by the provision of additional services.

Organizations such as the Australian Advisory Council on Bibliographic Services (AACOBS) and the LAA have been and are still involved in the development of a national information policy AACOBS, a co-operative body representing all types of libraries throughout Australia, has long been alerting librarians and others to the urgent need to establish such a policy. In 1978 AACOBS developed and published two statements on information policy designed for use at both the Federal and State level. Widely discussed and disseminated, the State level statement was adopted by Victoria. The approach was a somewhat narrow one and concentrated on information provision by libraries and their networks and the need to strengthen them by national co-ordination. AACOBS took the view that no individual or organization can function effectively in a modern society without access to information and that the availability of that information is the responsibility of the community and of the government.

In 1981 the ACT branch of the LAA held a seminar on national information policy which attracted a good deal of attention from both libraries and the bureaucracy. In 1983 the AACOBS annual national seminar was on 'NIP in an age of information technology' and again there was considerable interest. In 1984 the LAA made a submission on national information policy to the Minister for Science and Technology, and a draft statement on the subject is now under discussion at branch level. That statement raises issues of community access, education, communication, science and technology, industry and commerce, freedom of information, copyright, research and development and international links. The statement concludes:

The LAA believes that it is essential for Australia to develop a national information policy, adopt it and implement a national information plan based on that policy. The elements of such a plan should ensure the establishment of formal mechanisms of co-ordination between the various policies which together form the national information policy. Without such action Australia will not be able to develop satisfactorily as a democracy, with its citizens having access to and knowing how to access the information necessary for their work and leisure.[19]

The Australian Libraries and Information Council (ALIC) was established in 1981 to provide advice to governments at all levels on the development of library and related information services in Australia, especially on the creation of a national plan for library and related information services, and on the creation of mechanisms to facilitate resource sharing in libraries and information services.[20] ALIC prepared a document, *Plan for Library and Related Information Services in Australia*, which was circulated for comment in 1985. It is currently being revised and converted into a prescription for action. The plan stresses that adequate library services are essential to an informed nation and that present services are not adequate. Access to information must be available to all Australians. Any national information policy must be broadly based and flexible enough to accommodate rapid technological change.[21]

The most powerful boost that the policy received was its insertion in the ALP party platform in 1982. The statement was almost identical to the statement on *Information Policy: the need to know*, developed and adopted by the LAA in 1976. Revised later, the ALP policy is now less similar to that of the LAA. This was the first time that a political party had formally recognized the need for Australia to have a national information policy, centrally co-ordinated but operating at the Federal, State and local levels of government. As a direct result of that policy statement in the party platform, the present government established in 1983 an interdepartmental meeting to involve the Ministers of Science and Technology (now Science), Communications, Education and Youth Affairs (now Education) and Home Affairs and Environment (now Arts, Heritage and Environment) to prepare a plan for implementation of the policy.

In 1985 the Department of Science prepared a major discussion paper, 'A National Information Policy for Australia', and circulated it prior to a seminar conducted by the Department in December 1985.[22] The paper proposes the establishment of some form of advisory body to co-ordinate information activity not only within the Commonwealth government but between the Commonwealth and the States and local government and between the private and the public sectors. The concept remains to be worked out and the details are to be made available for wide comment.

At the seminar, several issues were identified as points of agreement or issues needing examination or action:
• the international value of information;
• collection of statistics about the information sector;
• cost recovery/charging for information versus equity of access;
• education for information use;
• information technology—threat or opportunity?;
• value of Telecom as a public monopoly;
• role of the media;
• information services to industry;
• scientific and technical information.[23]

Further refinement and discussion were necessary and in March 1986 a workshop on scientific and technological information (STI) was organized by the Department of Science. This had been identified as one of the areas needing urgent action and the workshop was designed to discuss the present state of scientific and technological information in Australia and to propose action for improvement. The establishment of an advisory institution/mechanism which would act as a co-ordinator for scientific and technological aspects of the wider national information policy was proposed. Neville Hurst in his summation stated the intention to bring to government for endorsement in late 1986 a set of guidelines together with recommendations for the formation of a consultative advisory and research body to advise government on information matters.[24]

Libraries have a strong interest in national information policy, as information is their business. With the introduction of information technology, libraries have become more closely interconnected with other groupings in the community. Decisions on communications policy now have a critical effect on libraries because so many use the communications network. Policies on the import of computer hardware and software, on trade practices, on transborder data flows, all directly affect libraries. The government has policies on some areas, such as copyright, communications, trade practices, imports/exports and freedom of information, but not in all relevant areas. It is possible for some aspects of these policies to be contradictory and they are certainly unco-ordinated. An overview is needed so that a coherent national approach to information can be achieved. Legislation will probably not be the result of the present deliberations, in fact it is hard to see how this would be helpful in such a volatile scene. A better solution would be a set of guidelines or perhaps a series of separate policies each describing different fields and each one complementing and supporting the other, forming part of Australia's national information policy.

ALIC, AACOBS and the LAA have done much to raise the level of awareness within library circles of the importance of and the need for a national information policy, and all three have contributed significantly to the discussions in the wider community. Librarians have been involved in the discussions organized by the Department of Science and must continue to be so involved. The end result of a national policy for Australia will be greater effectiveness and better co-ordination of information, and all libraries and their users will be the beneficiaries.

## A NEW FUTURE: ACCESS AND SERVICE POLICIES FOR LIBRARIES

In a country like Australia, with a few large centres of population and great distances, information technology has been a lifesaver. There are few limits now for remote users—mention has been made of the use of video-disc to make pictures available across vast distances and of CD-ROM to store economically large amounts of data. The geographical isolation of the Australian continent has been reduced by use of satellite communication—access to overseas data bases is a simple, direct and routine matter for all users on the continent. The new Parliament House in Canberra has been designed with a highly automated library and information system. Members' offices will each have a terminal linking them to the parliamentary library and to the electronic information systems in that library.

The possibilities for access to libraries through information technology are virtually limitless: the greatest difficulties will be in the cost of that access. How will the larger cost of access to the electronically stored information be paid for, and by whom? Governments have policies preventing any discrimination against specific groups of users, but libraries will have to pay for the cost of such access. It will be very tempting to solve the difficulty by charging the end user. A harder route but a more productive one will be to lobby funding sources and convince them that the right to free access to information is a fundamental democratic right and appropriate levels of funding must be made available. It is in fact imperative for libraries to take this route if our democratic society, based on an informed community, is to proceed into the twenty-first century.

Political barriers to access are a potential problem for libraries. Australia is very dependent on overseas data bases for information: these are largely held in Western countries. Australia would be vulnerable if a change in politics or in allies caused the bases to be closed. The Committee for Information, Computer and Communications Policy (ICCP) of OECD has been examining many of the issues arising from transborder data flows—the exchange of data across international boundaries—for some time. Limitations on what can be transmitted in or out of a country would have serious implications for Australian libraries and their users.

Given the transformation which information technology has brought to library services and administration, what will libraries do in the future, what do they need to do to ensure their survival? In an article called 'Look no paper! the library of tomorrow' a picture is drawn of a possible library of the future serviced by robots, stocked with talking books, video cassettes, computer programs, full text on microchips, terminals linked to remote data bases and facsimile machines.[25] The extended metaphor reads like science fiction, but as the author points out, the technology is available now. Although a somewhat chilling picture, it has some truth for the future; but most librarians believe that books, print and paper will be here for a long time, extensively supplemented by electronic devices. So too will libraries and librarians, to serve patrons in these institutions. Wainwright believes that changes in traditional library services will be likely to be in degree rather than kind. He predicts reduced use of print materials but greater use of other kinds of information formats. Like Veanor, Wainwright sees a much closer integration of the work of computer centres and libraries in the future.

It is important that the Library's facilitation role as a place of quiet study should not be forgotten and the Library is likely to remain a physical structure for this reason in any university with a sizeable number of graduate students . . . In the headlong rush into the arms of technology we should not forget the Library as a place of serious contemplation . . .[26]

Figures bandied around the library community state that 30 per cent of the local community use the public library yet 100 per cent pay for its establishment and upkeep. Other user figures vary, but examination of such statistics of libraries of all types would reveal that the potential market is far greater than the actual number of users. Libraries have a large potential market out there and must be more entrepreneurial, more active in promoting their resources and their services, their value to the community. Libraries must be more innovative in advertising services and in devising services which meet needs. Surprenant and Perry-Holmes state 'if librarians do not seize this initiative, there are profit-oriented entrepreneurs who will be anxious to skim the cream of the information market and reap the rewards'.[27]

There are categories of people who do not use libraries; for example, young unemployed make little use of libraries and their resources.

How can libraries serve their needs? What of services to the handicapped? Information technology provides the equipment for services to the blind, the deaf or the physically impaired, but such services are not as widespread as they should be. Other groups which have been neglected include the ethnic communities, the aged, the poor. Libraries can provide services to these groups and technology can assist, but funding authorities have to be convinced of the need to provide the appropriate resources.

With the increase in the amount of information available, it has become apparent that users want filtration and consolidation of the information they are offered. It is no longer enough to provide a list of references—some clients, especially business clients, want the actual answer. Such a trend raises questions of legal responsibility for librarians who inadvertently provide incorrect or inaccurate advice. Surprenant and Perry-Holmes predict reference services provided for a fee; but users will demand value for money.[28] Insurance against malpractice suits will be a future requirement. The High Court decision in the case of *Shaddock L. and Associates Pty Ltd* v. *Parramatta City Council* (1981) stated that government instrumentalities may be liable for damages where economic loss is sustained by persons acting on advice or information negligently provided by their officers. The case has been considered to have considerable implications for librarians as government employees offering advice to users. Some librarians are of the view that while all due care is taken they bear no responsibility for the accuracy or relevance of information. One wonders whether such a view can be sustained in the future.

Surprenant and Perry-Holmes see librarians acting as information consultants assisting users in the choice of a data base, designing a search strategy, organizing files and research data, choosing a computer and associated software and helping to 'debug' programs. This may well be on a fee-for-service basis. As more personal computers and terminals spread through the community the need to access the data will become independent of the hours of service which are attached to library buildings. A full range of specialized hotlines for quick answers on specific subjects will need to be provided.

The relevance of libraries to specific sectors in the community will need examination. Many of the business and industrial communities make only spasmodic use of libraries now, and access to data bases directly through vendors allows them to bypass libraries. Libraries will have to provide the fast and accurate services that business needs if they are to attract them as a client group. With increasing leisure and cheaper technological entertainments—video, compact disc, computer games—libraries as a source of recreation could fade away unless specific efforts are made to change services to meet the new needs of the community. Libraries have to learn to be more outgoing, to be innovative and imaginative in reaching their clientele. It will not be enough to rely on provision of good service—libraries have to shout loudly about that service and to reach out into different arenas to sell their services. It is a competitive market, but libraries using information technology can compete on equal terms with others in that market.

Veanor considers that 'no matter what technological advances occur within the next decade, human beings will continue to rely upon systems of recorded knowledge that reside in collections maintained by institutions dedicated to the preservation and communication of their contents to the community'.[29] Regardless of name or form of material, the institutions that maintain these collections will continue to be libraries. It is clear also that books and other printed materials will continue for some time to be the mainstay of library collections, supplemented or paralleled by the resources available through information technology.

The changes which information technology has brought to libraries in the last twenty years have been remarkable. The rapid development of information technology will continue, and impose consequent strains on libraries as they adapt their buildings, their staff, equipment and services to those changes. The problems imposed by those changes outlined in this paper are far from insoluble. Information technology has provided libraries with a unique opportunity for the provision of better services to the ultimate benefit of the community.

# PART III

# State Policies

# CHAPTER 9

# INFORMATION TECHNOLOGY AND MICRO-ELECTRONICS IN VICTORIA*

## SIGNIFICANCE OF INFORMATION TECHNOLOGY

Information technology is becoming increasingly important with the convergence of micro-electronics, computing and telecommunications. Information is an essential input into every aspect of economic decision-making and the foundation upon which a market economy, modern government and society is built.

Information technology draws on developments in micro-electronics and includes:
• computing hardware;
• computing software;
• advanced computing systems;
• information data bases;
• business automation;
• local area networks;
• telecommunications.
Progressively, as technology allows, all information is being converted into digital electronic form—visual, sound and written. This will enable greater networking and for information to be integrated, analysed and presented in totally new ways.

Manufacturing and service industries in Victoria and Australia generally will depend increasingly on the speed and efficiency of information networks. These networks will become to the future what transport systems have been to the past.

Advances in micro-electronics technology have made information technology one of the fastest growing and most dynamic industry sectors, with worldwide growth rates between 10 and 30 per cent forecast.

Such growth will occur in Australia and overseas irrespective of local industry developments. It is vitally important for Victoria to

---

Reprinted from Economic Strategy for Victoria Statement No. 8, *Technology Statement*, Victorian Government July 1986 ensure that it has a strong information technology capability so that it can gain not just from the use of information technology but also by manufacturing and providing information technology products and services.

Initiatives described below are designed to assist in developing the capacity of local industry to share in this global growth. Government, as a significant user and purchaser of information technology, can benefit local industry to a significant extent. The initiatives being undertaken have the dual objective of developing local capability and assisting local industry to grow through exports.

The Australian information processing market was estimated to exceed $7 billion in 1986 with growth to $13 billion predicted by 1990. Much of this growth has occurred in the computer hardware industry. Over the last three years there has been a growth of 20 per cent in mainframe, 30 per cent in mini-computer, and 80 per cent in micro-computer installations in Australia. About 35 per cent of these computers have been bought by governments. Australian computer hardware revenues are estimated to exceed $3 billion in 1986.

Many of the thirty-eight local manufacturers of personal computers or components are either wholly owned subsidiaries of foreign companies assembling in Australia, or joint ventures between Australian and foreign manufacturers producing machines in Australia. Some local companies produce enhancements and compatibles for well-known foreign computer manufacturers.

Although it is sometimes difficult for locally owned companies to keep pace with global technological improvements, the success of the locally owned company Labtam Pty Ltd in producing computers of its own design and development is an excellent example.

The Australian software service industry exceeded $1 billion in revenue in 1986, and is growing at about 20 per cent per annum. Victoria has 40 per cent of Australian software establishments, and the ability to capitalize internationally on its indigenous strengths.

The growth of public-access data bases in Australia has been spectacular in recent years. Major public access networks include Ausinet, Csironet, Clirs, ICL Videotex, Infonet, IP Sharp, Viatel and Maynenet. The Victorian data-base industry is very active and capable of further significant expansion at producer, vendor and user levels.

The merging of telecommunications with the information-processing power of computers is only beginning. Satellites, fibre optic networks and the conversion of the telephone network to a digital transmission system will form the basic network infrastructure. Many new devices will be added to the network, including facsimile, computers, videotext, electronic mail and teleconferencing. Already in Australia services such as computer sale of livestock are at the forefront of advanced technology applications.

Telecommunications and computing advances are converging with significant benefits to business automation. The Australian office automation market has just exceeded $1 billion per annum and has enormous growth potential. This growth is occurring in digital tele-phone switchboards, dedicated word processors, specialized com-puter workstations, new office automation software and dedicated hardware processors and local area networks (communication loops interconnecting a set of workstations and computers into a single network).

In all areas of information technology there are opportunities to develop local expertise and production to capitalize on the high growth potential.

## MICRO-ELECTRONICS

The base upon which information technology is built is micro-elec-tronics. The rapid development of micro-electronic technology is having a major impact on both the manufacturing and information industries throughout the world. Reduced sizes and increased power of micro-electronic components have led to an explosion in computing hardware and telecommunications capabilities.

Micro-electronics is one of the largest and fastest growing industries in the world and in Australia. Successful participation in micro-elec-tronics is a prerequisite for growth in manufacturing generally, as has been seen in all countries with a viable manufacturing base.

Micro-electronics has two fundamental aspects. One is a design function where specialized circuits are created to measure, control, calculate and display the operations of equipment ranging from re-frigerators to oceanographic research devices. The other major aspect is the development of further applications for newly emerging circuit designs.

Micro-electronic applications offer substantial cost efficiencies. Consequently, large-scale investments are being made in the United States, Japan and Europe to capture these gains. Victoria's task will be to match these developments with our industrial capacity, needs and skills. There are three principal areas of manufacture within micro-electronics—electronic components, electronic equipment and circuit boards.

### Electronic components

The world micro-electronic component market consists mainly of:
- integrated circuits or digital chips;
- hybrid devices which combine thick-film analogue techniques with thin-film digital chips, and
- semiconductor transducers.

Fabrication of thin-film integrated circuits takes place only in South Australia and New South Wales; Australian R & D in this area is insig-nificant by world standards. However, there has been a surge of interest in Australia in design, and a number of tertiary education institutions and various companies now have design expertise in advanced micro-electronic circuits. In the hybrid chip field there is considerable commercial activity, no doubt because the 'entrance fee' to this technology is a fraction of that in the integrated circuit field. Contract design services and experimental facilities are available for companies in this area. Whilst the manufacture and sale of chips or semiconductor devices dominates the international business of micro-electronics—large corporations such as Intel, Motorola and National Semiconductor share a market approaching $25 billion in value—few semiconductors are made in Australia.

### Electronic equipment

Whilst Australia's indigenous electronic equipment industry has been in decline over the last decade, there has been considerable research and development undertaken by academic and government institutions. Disappointingly, much of this work has failed to be communicated to, and/or adopted, by local companies. AWA is the only Australian-owned electronics company of any appreciable size and covers a wide field—radio, computing, telecommunications, avionics and electronic instrumentation. However, many new and entrepreneurial firms are developing electronic equipment using the flexibility of micro-electronics to create new products and new markets. However, these firms are often inhibited by our poor infrastructure in electronic components and circuit-board manufacture.

### Circuit boards

High-quality, single-layer conventional circuit boards are designed and manufactured under contract or in house by many equipment companies in many locations in Australia. Perhaps the most modern is the Ericsson facility in Broadmeadows. Victorian-based manufacturers such as Printronics also provide excellent facilities.

There are, however, very limited facilities available for users who are looking for large-volume production, or who want the advanced circuit boards now being incorporated into overseas electronic products. These new circuit boards have many active layers and are themselves being reduced in size with developments such as surface mounting of chips, use of active elements in the board itself and use of ceramic and other new materials.

## OPPORTUNITIES FOR VICTORIA

To capture the maximum benefits for Victoria, industry and government must keep pace with global developments. There is scope to capitalize on local strengths particularly in computer software and electronic equipment. Many technologies which will not be developed here can be introduced by industrial co-operation and strategic partnering in world markets. Some Victorian companies currently have valuable links with major international organizations.

Victoria has significant strengths in micro-electronics in that a number of Australia's principal integrated-circuit designers are based in Melbourne. Their skill in advanced design is in demand internationally. It is this skills resource, widely spread throughout the industry, which provides the base for growth of this technology sector in Victoria. The Centre for Micro-electronic Applications and the Micro-electronics Technology Centre at RMIT provide both an R & D and commercial face to innovation in this area. Several research companies involved in data communications and manipulation, as well as scientific instruments and control devices, have designed their own micro-electronic applications for export-based products.

Victoria is also fortunate in having a large number of entrepreneurial and rapidly expanding export-oriented micro-electronic equipment companies in the fields of computers (e.g., Webster Computers, Labtam International and Datacraft Australia), electronic equipment (e.g., BWD Instruments, Nilsen Electrical Industries) and networks (O'Dowd Research).

Scientific control equipment and metering devices are all manufactured here. Computer peripherals, advanced circuit boards and custom-made devices are designed and built in Victoria and actively marketed abroad. The government has been an active supporter of many of these companies, either by way of direct commercial assistance or marketing support.

Whilst most of Victoria's approximately two hundred electronics companies are relatively small and undercapitalized, they provide a basis for Victoria's growth. The Department of Industry, Technology and Resources has extended a number of support services to such companies to overcome these difficulties.

Whilst most of the computer hardware and software market is dominated by imports, there is greater scope for development of the local software industry. High growth rates, low entry costs and local industry expertise provide a sound basis for future growth domestically and internationally. The local software industry has some strengths which can be built on. Victorian and Australian companies are highly skilled and experienced in the development of English-language software.

In the highly competitive computer hardware and telecommunications area, the development of international partnerships provides an opportunity to keep pace with global technological development and for local firms to gain access to world markets. This will, as is evident already, serve to stimulate and provide confidence to indigenous designers and developers. There is scope for commercialization of Victorian based research, particularly in telecommunications through the expertise of Telecom and its research facility at Clayton. The new CSIRO Division of Information Technology is to establish a specialist communications group in Melbourne, thus creating an even greater potential for private-sector activity.

There are over twenty researchers at Victorian tertiary institutions undertaking research in aspects of advanced computing such as artificial intelligence. This follows a global trend of large research investment in fifth-generation computers, fourth-generation languages, artificial intelligence and expert systems. Although development times can be lengthy, this is an area where intellectual investment will generate world market opportunities.

As telecommunications, computers and office products converge, a wealth of opportunities are created. The challenge for Victoria is not only to design and develop local area networks, smart phones and the like, but to incorporate these developments to increase production and service efficiency.

Whilst the majority of growth in information technology will ensue from the private sector, government can have a significant role in supporting major technology development applications. As a user, government can apply its purchasing power to strengthen local development and accelerate the application and development of new products and services in information technology. Major areas where government support can assist firms is in encouraging international partnerships, creation of educational and training opportunities, strengthening research commercialization processes and assistance with product, process and market development.

## MAJOR INITIATIVES

### Software publishing organizations

In 1985 the government announced support for the establishment of one or more commercially viable organizations to publish and market Victorian software internationally. In February 1986, 250 invitations were sent to Victorian and interstate businesses seeking responses to a detailed position paper. Some fifteen proposals were received from thirty companies (mainly independent software houses). Two proposals were selected for detailed analysis and negotiation. Both proposals involve the establishment of software publishing operations to focus particularly on export markets, beginning with North America. Software products in both enterprises will be derived both from within the structure of the respective companies and from other independent Australian software authors.

The first proposal was received from Computer Power Pty Ltd. The government has reached agreement with Computer Power to contribute equity capital of $4.67 million in return for a 40 per cent equity holding. This investment by the government will facilitate the establishment of a software publishing organization and the acquisition of an existing US-based software company with marketing and distribution outlets in the USA and Europe.

The second proposal was received from Integrity Management Services Pty Ltd, Tritek Pty Ltd and Caple Bryce Pty Ltd. Negotiations are well advanced between the government and these companies for the establishment of a second major software publishing facility in Victoria.

## Electronic libraries and data bases

The government operates at all levels of the data-base industry. It is a producer of vast information and one of the largest users of information. This central role in the industry led the Victorian government to commission a consultancy to examine the opportunities for government data-base retailing.

The study identified three main areas of potential:
- more efficient satisfaction of existing high-volume commercial information needs;
- release of information that is presently restricted; and
- better dissemination of information about government and its processes, particularly where that information is likely to change.

The detailed content of the consultant's report is currently being analysed. This work is being co-ordinated by the recently created Division of Information Technology in the Department of Management and Budget.

## Telecommunications

Following receipt of a report on telecommunications policy from a Victorian government task force chaired by the Honourable M. J. Sandon M.P., the Victorian government established a ministerial committee in March 1986 to undertake a major telecommunications initiative.

The project has two main purposes:
- to develop a long-term strategy plan for the planning, provision and management of telecommunications facilities for Victorian government departments and statutory authorities; and
- to recommend to government a range of initiatives designed to encourage the growth of a stronger and more export-oriented telecommunications industry in Victoria.

Phase one of the telecommunications planning study addressed the present and future telecommunications needs of Victorian government users. This investigation highlighted the fact that there is considerable scope to improve the cost-effectiveness of the government's use of telecommunication services and to benefit the community directly through the delivery of improved and new services to the public.

In phase two of the study consultants were commissioned to prepare proposals to meet the identified needs of the Victorian public sector for telecommunications facilities. As a key objective of the telecommunications project is to encourage the development of Victorian industry in this field, the phase two study proposals were to take account of the impact on local industry and its export capability.

The ministerial committee recommended to the government, on 30 June 1986, a number of initiatives aimed at overcoming barriers or obstacles to the future development of the telecommunications industry in Victoria.

## O'Dowd Research networking system

O'Dowd Research Pty Ltd is a small local company which is developing radically new integrated-data voice communications technology of potential international significance. The government has agreed to provide capital in return for a minority equity position in O'Dowd Research.

The technology developed by this company involves a new local and wide-area networking system which allows different computer terminals and host computers to be connected together without having to be programmed by the user. The system uses hardware protocol conversion techniques instead of the more conventional software conversion.

## Chip fabrication and design facilities

A major initiative has been to establish an integrated-circuit final-stage chip fabrication facility working to minimum micron industry standards and offering semi-custom design facilities especially suited to gate array devices. RMIT and the Centre for Industrial Micro-electronic Applications are working closely with the government to develop this important proposal. The design skills available at these centres are of world standard and when matched with a selective fabrication resource will represent a vital initiative in this crucial industry.

This proposal reveals the dilemma which must be addressed by potential participants in this industry. Broad-scale manufacturing of standard components is extremely expensive. Consequently, decisions by governments to invest are usually made at the national level. Overseas, such facilities have been created in an effort to overtake a perceived 'technology lag' and become competitive. The dilemma is that to not participate in the micro-electronics fabrication industry excludes investment in a technology which is equal in its historical impact to the introduction of steam power. Not to invest is to turn away from one of the major sources of future industrial growth.

The solution to this dilemma is to make a selective investment such as that described above with the integrated-circuit final-stage fabrication plant. The lead times and returns on this investment will be medium-term and dependent on aggressive marketing in a highly competitive market.

The proposal to establish such a fabrication plant has been welcomed by several large corporations which have expressed a desire to make a strategic investment in this area. The government believes that both overseas investors and the State's citizens can gain from this development. It promises a substantial base for earnings and profits as well as a skills platform and educational resource for the future of Victoria's workers.

## New ferro-electric memory chip facility

Another major initiative under consideration at present involves possible participation by the government in a Victorian venture sponsored by Newtech Development Corporation.

Newtech is a listed Australian company involved in the commercialization of a major new memory device being developed in conjunction with the University of Colorado at Colorado Springs. The new Australian company will manufacture the memory chip, known as 'Rampac', under licence to Ramtron Corporation, Newtech's US-based micro-electronics subsidiary. The Rampac memory chip is a device which has the potential to operate at speeds 10 000 times faster than existing comparable memory capacity devices. The potential demand for Rampac is estimated to be hundreds of millions of dollars. Because of its advanced features and non-volatility, the Rampac chip will gain immediate entry into the worldwide integrated-circuit memory market. These memory chips would be used in motor vehicles, computers, telecommunications, satellites and aerospace applications. The Victorian venture will draw heavily on research and development capacities at RMIT, which is a leader in gallium arsenide technology. (Gallium arsenide is a new material which improves on the silicon-based devices which have been the industry standard.)

The government is also developing a proposal for an advanced-circuit packaging facility in Victoria. Such a service will underpin many of the entrepreneurial electronic companies in the State.

## FURTHER DEVELOPMENTS

### Micro-electronics

The Victorian government is actively seeking to encourage micro-electronic developments which are growth-oriented, dependent on advanced skills, involve the manufacture of high-value-added products and have export potential. A key objective in this area is the achievement of international industry standards. There is no place for outdated technologies and standards.

The Victorian government has received three detailed reports on the micro-electronics industry.

One of the reports, from RMIT, concentrated on evolving technologies and mechanisms for commercializing these opportunities. This review contributed towards the plan for a focused integrated-circuit design and fabrication facility. It also highlighted the demands made on personnel and skills resources and on the caution required in developing an industry strategy in electronics.

A second report, by Hardie Technologies, commented on the creative and management implications of adopting micro-electronic applications in Australia. New product development and exploitation of the industry's strengths (including the uses of 'transferred' technologies) were highlighted in this report.

The third report, by the Centre for Micro-electronic Applications, concentrated on commercial applications of micro-electronics and analysed the basis of the industry in Victoria. This valuable report suggested which industry sectors might be most amenable to microelectronic applications in measurement, control, display and calculation.

Advice has also been sought from PA Technology on strategic directions in micro-electronics.

World-class product standards and manufacturing efficiency is essential to achieve medium- to long-term growth in this industry. The government is committed to making available its several industry programmes to stimulate micro-electronic developments.

## Computer hardware

Recognizing that the best commercial opportunities are in developing a 'total solution' approach using systems, software and marketing skills, two opportunities are being developed at present:

- a joint venture between a local software company and a Japanese hardware company, to take local software, provide the translation interface and market direct into Japan;
- a joint venture between Australian hardware and software firms to tackle markets for specific applications domestically and internationally.

The Victorian government recognizes the importance of its own purchasing policies on the computer hardware industry. To this end, agreement has been reached to abolish State purchasing preferences which have encouraged greater fragmentation in the industry. The new National Preference Agreement took effect on 1 July 1986. The government has introduced the approved supplier policy which should simplify the provision of hardware to government. Computer hardware suppliers will have equal opportunity to be selected as preferred suppliers. The Victorian government will maintain its offsets policy, which applies to purchases of imported computer hardware, and is continuing negotiations with the Federal government to ensure greater commonality between the two respective offsets schemes.

## Software industry

The Victorian government is also conscious of the need to ensure that the production side of the software industry is encouraged, particularly in leading areas of technological development.

While the new software publishing operations will assist the production of quality software by commissioning product and maintaining high review standards, more action is needed. Specifically, there is a need to foster greater product development. Accordingly, the Victorian government is planning the establishment of an advanced software development business. Again, such a business must be commercial but would operate on a long payback cycle. It would foster product conceptualization through appropriate mechanisms and ensure product development through assistance with development tools and working capital. The government is working closely with Intelligent Systems Research Pty Ltd, among others, on this initiative. In addressing the advanced software market the government is confident that local firms can take advantage of the market opportunities currently available. Should product be successfully developed, software marketing mechanisms will be available to export to overseas markets.

The Victorian government considers the software industry to be a key element in its industry development strategy. Consistent with this a number of further initiatives are being pursued, viz:
• a computing industry advisory committee;
• promotion of a single software industry association;
• specific export promotion programmes; and
• encouragement of training and education.

## Business automation

Little information is available on Australian manufacture of office automation systems. Some manufacture of micro-computers (which use imported word-processing packages) occurs, together with local manufacture of modems.

To obtain more data on this industry the Department of Industry, Technology and Resources is helping to sponsor a study of future trends in office automation in Australia, to be co-ordinated by the Australian Office Automation Council. The study will specifically consider commercial opportunities for local producers in the office automation market. The Department of Industry, Technology and Resources is investigating the feasibility of assisting a joint venture of local companies in providing products and systems. Of relevance is the opportunity to develop such a joint venture on the basis of government business but with a firm view to export-proven products and systems.

# CHAPTER 10

# INFORMATION TECHNOLOGY POLICY IN WESTERN AUSTRALIA

## Geoffrey Layzell Ward

It was appropriate that Western Australia won the America's Cup in 1983: the Cup was won because technology was applied to the design of the yacht and also because the winning team used advanced information technology to keep abreast of the performance of the teams whilst the race was actually taking place.

Western Australia has been so keen to use information technology that it has not waited to work out a *formal* information technology policy for the State. There are, however, a number of announced principles, and ministers of the State government have made a number of statements on the subject.

Western Australia firmly believes that it is among the leaders in Australia in accepting and even embracing the introduction of IT, and is benefiting economically from having done so, despite not having a formal IT policy. Its policies have resulted in some companies active in information technology starting in Western Australia, for example, Olivetti, AT&T, Circuit Technology. Unfortunately the information technology industry is not recognized as a discrete area in the Federal government's statistics; it is covered in a number of other categories including 'electronics'. However, it seems likely that a significant proportion of this category is in fact information technology. In the field of electronics, exports from Western Australia rose from 12 per cent of sales in 1979 to 35 per cent in 1984.[1]

## WESTERN AUSTRALIA'S TECHNOLOGY PROGRAMME 1983–

The appointment of a Minister of Technology in 1983 was an indication of the positive approach of the government to technology. This was followed up by the passing of the Technology Development Act in December 1983.

## The Technology Development Act

The Technology Development Act established the Technology Directorate, the Technology Development Authority, and the Science, Industry and Technology Council (SITCO).

When introducing the Act into Parliament, Mr Bryce, the Minister of Technology (now Minister of Technology and Industry) said:

The Bill recognises that the Government has a significant role to play in enabling the State—both the private and public sectors—to meet the challenge facing us all.

. . . technological changes are impacting on every aspect of our lives, not just at work, but also at home, in our family and personal lives.

. . . The Government's aim is as follows—

Firstly, to show the way; leadership in the community; to demonstrate to others by example that the Government has faith and hope in the future of technology in this State.

Secondly, to promote private and Government sector co-operation and consensus; to establish mechanisms by which the various stakeholders in the State can come together and share their ideas on the future.

Thirdly, planning for the future; to take a strategic view on the long-term goals or desired outcomes from technology; to take steps to co-ordinate and mobilise resources, and point them in the right direction.[2]

The Technology Development Authority (an incorporated body) was created to promote technology parks and the commercialization of technology (especially *high* technology).

The Technology Directorate provides 'think-tank' research in technology and co-ordinates technology policy.

SITCO was established as an advisory body of specialists, appointed on a part-time basis, to advise the State government on developments in the fields of science, industry and technology. The membership of the Council is selected both to have appropriate expertise, and to be representative of the community. SITCO has a chairman and a full-time executive officer located at the Technology Directorate, and the Directorate provides the secretarial and administrative services required by the Council. The executive director of the Technology Directorate is also an ex-officio member of SITCO. The Council has established a number of working parties, often with the executive officer as convenor. Topics covered include:

• Western Australian Science and Technology Centre;
• space-related industries;
• energy technology;
• social and industrial impact of technology;
• information technology;
• minerals industry;
• innovation and intellectual property.

## Finance

As one of the major requisites for the nurture of a new venture is a source of finance and of financial advice, a number of bodies have been established by (or have at the least the moral support of) the government. One example is the Technology Development Fund.

## The Western Australian Technology Park

The Western Australian Technology Park was was opened in July 1985. The purpose of this Park is to provide nursery facilities for new ventures and an appropriate environment for high-technology companies. The Park provides design and testing facilities, and organizations capable of offering finance and advice on legal matters are located there.

## Technology transfer

It is the policy of the Western Australian government to stimulate technology transfer as one of the methods of ensuring the highest possible standards of technology within the State. The government has purchased a number of mainframe computers from IBM and Amdahl, and the Department of Computing and Information Technology (DOCIT) has, as part of that contract, negotiated a $15 million benefits package for local industry. (In negotiating the supply of terminal equipment for use with these computers, DOCIT took into account the technology transfer activities of the vendors within the State. IT is obviously not the only field where this principle is likely to be applied in the future.)

## Education and training

The Western Australian government has funded a number of training initiatives in the field of information technology. For example:
- traineeships are being operated by DOCIT for the benefit of 100 unemployed young people for a period of six months;
- the same department is involved in the organization of the Federally funded ITechs, modelled on the well-known and very successful system started in Notting Dale in the UK;
- the Small Business Development Corporation has conducted some seminars on the use of new technology, and inevitably this is mainly information technology;
- guidelines have been produced for the introduction of information technology into local government.

Areas of future action have been identified by the Information Technology Study which is described later in this chapter.

## COMMUNITY INVOLVEMENT

The government has received useful advice from SITCO on information technology, in the form of a report based largely on consultative discussions with the community. An edited version of this report has now been published, and this is described in detail below. The Technology Directorate organizes a series of meetings called SIT forums, some of which are on the subject of information technology, and these have been attended by over 3000 people. Information Technology Month, a series of public awareness activities organized once a year and lasting for about a month, has received financial and administrative support from the State as well as from other sources.

## ESTABLISHMENT OF THE DEPARTMENT OF COMPUTING AND INFORMATION TECHNOLOGY (DOCIT)

DOCIT, the first department of its kind in Australia, drew much of its personnel from the computer section of Treasury. The establishment of the Department was announced by the Honourable Mal Bryce, in Parliament on 15 November 1984. To quote from *Hansard*:

Mr BRYCE: Western Australia is developing a reputation nationally and internationally for initiative and vigour in the fields of applied science and technology.

The State is now gearing up for the new era in information technology by setting up Australia's first department dealing solely with computing and information technology.

... the Department of Computing and Information Technology will pursue the following objectives as outlined in the corporate plan—

To assure the effective and efficient use of information technology in the Western Australian public sector,

to facilitate the effective and efficient development of Western Australian public sector information systems,

to facilitate the efficient operation of Western Australian public sector information systems,

to promote technology awareness and the use of information technology across Western Australia ...

This Government is committed to utilising information technology to facilitate the diversification of the economic base of this State and ultimately to improve the living standards of all Western Australians.[3]

## DEVELOPMENT OF THE WESTERN AUSTRALIAN INFORMATION TECHNOLOGY POLICY

Development of the State's Information Technology policy was prompted by the well-publicized claims of a number of eminent persons and by articles in both the professional and popular press that some developed nations had undergone a revolution akin to the agricultural and industrial revolutions, culminating, so far as Australia was concerned, in Barry Jones' book, *Sleepers Wake!*.[4] SITCO suggested to the Minister of Technology that information technology should be the subject of an investigation by the Council. The Minister of Technology endorsed this suggestion and the Council therefore started to make arrangements for the project which has come to be known as the Western Australian Information Technology Study.

## The Western Australian Information Technology Study

Annemie Gilbert, a member of SITCO and an information professional, was recruited on secondment from the Western Australian
Institute of Technology to commence work on the investigation.
SITCO set up a working party to oversee the project. The working
party consisted of a number of other professionals who were selected
for their expertise not only in information and information technology
but also in the management of investigations. The Western Australian
Technology Directorate took an active role in the investigations and
provided much of the funding to cover the cost of employing consultants. ACCESS Computing Consultants and the Centre for Applied
Business Research were awarded contracts to assist with the investigations and the working party was strengthened by representatives
from these two organizations.

The working party set itself the primary objective of recommending
policies and supporting strategies which would promote and foster the
most beneficial, effective and efficient use of information and information technology in WA, in both the public and private sectors. The
working party's definition of 'information' was 'item(s) of knowledge,
item(s) of data, control parameter(s)'; for the purposes of the study the
qualification 'which are manipulatable by information technology'
was added. This leads immediately to the question of what is
information technology. The conclusion was that whilst the term
'information technology' was inherently general, today 'information
technology' has the narrower connotation of electronic and/or optical
technology, with the specific implication of the use of computers and
telecommunications.

The study obtained data from four sources:
- a literature search;
- a questionnaire which was sent to members of the technology
  industry;
- a series of structured interviews with representative members of all
  sections of the community;
- extensive interviews with a small number of experts.

For the interviews, a list of occupations was prepared, derived in
part from Australian Bureau of Statistics occupational categories.
From this a further list was prepared of people who were representative of these different groups and these were then interviewed. In
addition, appropriate managers from departments of the Federal, State
and local governments were interviewed. Other groups interviewed
were representatives of trade unions, voluntary agencies, professional
bodies and so on. The experts in the first list were: Professor Michael
Scriven of the Education Department of the University of Western
Australia, an expert on the use of computers in education who is also
very knowledgeable about information technology; Professor Don
Lamberton from the Economics Department of the University of
Queensland; Professor Francis Auburn from the University of
Western Australia Faculty of Law. These specialist consultants sup-

plied the background knowledge necessary for informed interpretation of the results.

The industry survey questionnaire was carefully worded to obtain information about the status, strengths, weaknesses and needs of the information technology industry, and notwithstanding the low response rate of 23 per cent gave very useful and consistent answers. A number of firms which responded were interviewed by phone in order to amplify some of their answers: these conversations were noted and added to the material obtained by interview.

The survey was designed to find out:
- the range of activities from which information industry revenue was earned;
- market segments served;
- the competitive position of the firm, as perceived by the firm itself;
- marketing sales history and activity;
- expectation of growth;
- manpower demographics and skill levels;
- research and development activities;
- attitudes towards the role and activities of government.

(IBM declined to respond to the survey, but did agree to take part in the interviews.)

## The results

The results of the questionnaire showed that firms operating in the information technology industry had histories of high rates of growth, and that they had high expectations of growth. The industry is thought to be technically competent; sales people's knowledge of the products they were selling was unsatisfactory in some cases; financial and marketing skills were not thought to be good. The industry felt that the government did not give it sufficient recognition, and wanted a more supportive fiscal and legal environment. It felt that help was needed with marketing overseas, possibly on the mentor principle or with help from government. The industry wanted government contracting changed so as to help the small but technically competent. There were critical shortages of skilled staff, and especially of staff skilled in management or marketing *and* with technical knowledge of information technology.

The costs of telecommunications were said to be significantly restricting the use of information technology, and whence to be impeding desirable business techniques. In particular the criticism was made that dial-up facilities including Viatel were being used in preference to the dedicated lines that users would prefer. The suggestion was made that two or more firms could share a line, and that Telecom should change its rules to permit this, after the 'half-a-loaf is better than no bread' principle. The alternative suggestion was direct subsidy, on the basis that (Western) Australia had legitimate geographical reasons for subsidizing communications, and that overseas governments used subsidy to overcome problems of this nature.

On employment the study found that information technology has had a marked effect, in both directions. On the one hand, it has led to structural unemployment and increased productivity without corresponding increases in employment; but on the other hand, information technology has led to the survival of firms that would otherwise not have been able to continue, with consequent preservation of employment, and has provided significant new employment. The net result is an employment gain.

One effect of the rapid development of technology, and information technology in particular, is that there is a strong possibility that in a working lifetime, people may have to have more than one type of job. This will clearly need to be reflected in the education process, where the student will have to be made aware of this possibility, and where retraining will need to be introduced, to introduce the new skills and to upgrade old skills. It will have to be reflected in different social attitudes—such changes will have to be accepted as the norm. Methods will have to be developed to provide financial support for those being retrained, including householders.

In the area of education, participants in the study thought that the tertiary sector was performing well in training those students learning information technology. The institutions are expected to remain in the forefront of developments (although this relies on the acquisition of new and expensive equipment whilst under current financial constraints). The salaries that are paid to staff are lower than they can obtain in the market place.

It was acknowledged that the primary and secondary sectors are aware of information technology, and are trying to fulfil their obligations. However it was felt that they are more interested in the insides of the boxes than in their use as a tool. School-leavers were perceived as being 'computer-literate' but this may be merely a reflection of the presence of computers in schools, rather than an accurate comment about students' competence.

The study highlighted the fact that whilst younger people are aware of and familiar with the technology, this is not so true for older people. There is a need to provide retraining courses for all those qualified in other areas who now need information technology skills. Courses for middle and senior management are urgently required.

The handicapped can benefit enormously from information technology, but the equipment is not yet approved for exemption from tax imposts, as are for example special cars. Welfare groups find it difficult to obtain the information that they require from government departments because they do not know where to get it. This also applies to a lesser extent to the general public, especially those in remote locations, who also find the costs of obtaining information restrictive.

Among legal issues arising from the expansion of information technology are copyright and privacy protection. It was felt that copyright should be applicable to the information carried rather than the medium by which it is conveyed: this would include all future developments. Backup copies of software should be permitted in a controlled fashion, i.e., in a manner laid down in the Act: this would be prone to abuse but perhaps not more so than at present. As for privacy, this is an area of strong feelings. People are frightened of those holding their personal data taking advantage of that possession. The other feeling which emerged is that data bases of private information are getting too large, and that electronic data bases are much more accessed than the same data on paper. The working party urged that consideration should be given to making it unlawful, unless consent has been given, to sell private data such as planning consents and subscription lists. All individuals should be entitled to know of any personal data held about them, with the right to compel correction of proven error, and with the right to enforce transfer, for example, on removal, migration, change of medical practitioner, etc., and must give their consent before data can be transferred. A commissioner should be appointed to oversee these regulations.

The study concluded that Western Australia is grasping the opportunities offered by the information revolution, but it does have problems because of its geographical isolation and population distribution.

SITCO and DOCIT are now obtaining reactions from the community to the study, and as reported DOCIT is working on a public-sector IT policy. The all-pervasiveness of IT within the community is such that regardless of the government in power, the policy has to be very carefully worked out.

## CONCLUSIONS

The Western Australian information technology policy is therefore likely to include the following objectives:

- to establish an environment in which information technology can be used to the greatest benefit of the Western Australian society/economy;
- to promote the most effective and efficient use of information technology within the Western Australian public sector;
- to encourage the effective and efficient use of information technology within the Western Australian private sector;
- to co-ordinate the use of information technology within the public sector, and the co-ordination of purchasing, servicing and maintenance so that, subject to considerations of privacy, there is minimal duplication of operations;
- to ensure that information technology is not operated within either the public or private sectors in a manner that conflicts with the rights, privacy and just aspirations of the community;
- to improve the performance of all sectors of the community by the

improved supply of information, and to improve the accuracy of that information.

Additional considerations which may be added are:

- the geographical features of Western Australia are such that information technology will be used to reduce the isolation and other difficulties of those who live in remote areas;
- information technology could also be used as a means of reducing the burdens of the disabled.

# PART IV

# International Information Issues

# CHAPTER 11

# TRANSBORDER DATA FLOWS AND NATIONAL SOVEREIGNTY*

## John Langdale

Reports on international economic, political, sporting and cultural events in the daily news on television and in the newspapers remind us that we live in a highly interdependent world. Australia's and other countries' international linkages are intensifying. The ever-expanding web of international trade, legal, diplomatic and other agreements have many positive impacts, but they also have the effect of constraining the individual countries' governments in their freedom to make decisions. Thus global interdependency limits national sovereignty.

Growth of international information flows has paralleled expansion of these global linkages. Few people are aware of the massive growth in the volume of business and financial information that is transferred internationally via electronic and other means of communication. Even fewer are aware of the nature of the economic, political and social changes that have resulted from these developments. This chapter focuses on one aspect of these changes: the national sovereignty issue.

The emergence of an international information economy is creating new benefits and dangers for countries. Some have argued that such a world economy will benefit all; global communications networks and rapid adoption of information technologies will reduce disparities in living standards. These developments will also minimize barriers of distance, which have inhibited communications for economic and social purposes.

Others see these developments in a less favourable light. They argue that the spread of new telecommunications and other information technologies is unlikely to benefit all countries; inequalities in access to information are likely to increase. Diffusion of new information technologies will enhance dominance-dependency relationships, for

---

*Several sections of this chapter are based on material contained in a report to the Department of Communications: J. V. Langdale, *Transborder Data Flow and International Trade in Electronic Information Services: An Australian Perspective*, Australian Government Publishing Service, Canberra, 1985.

it is the major industrialized countries that will benefit most from these developments. Many countries are concerned about their emerging dependency on foreign sources of information and information-processing facilities. The national sovereignty issue in international telecommunications and information technologies has arisen in a number of countries: these include Third World countries in general, and France, Canada, Sweden, and Australia.[1] Paradoxically, the US has also been concerned about loss of national sovereignty, despite its commanding technological lead in many areas in the production of information equipment (electronics, computers and telecommunications) and information services. This fear is partly related to the rise of Japan as a major competitor in sectors of information equipment manufacture. The US government perceives information technology in general, and international telecommunications in particular, as vital to the US's continued role as a world power.[2]

This chapter examines the nature of the shift into an international information economy. A number of factors leading to this shift are considered: demand for international information transfer, technological change and government policy. As Australia is linked to the international information economy, a key issue is: to what extent is the Australian economy vulnerable to disruption from international sources? Is this vulnerability likely to increase in the future?

While the chapter focuses on national sovereignty concerns, it is important not to assume that the negative effects of these linkages to the international information economy outweigh the advantages. It is not possible in this chapter to consider fully the relative advantages and disadvantages of such linkages.

## INTERNATIONAL TRADE IN SERVICES

International telecommunications issues are becoming increasingly intertwined with those in the area of trade in services. Services which rely on telecommunications and electronic information systems (EIS) are being increasingly traded internationally. EISs can be divided into two categories. Primary EISs include firms whose main function is in the handling of electronic forms of information; they operate, for example, in banking, finance, computer services, electronic media (television and radio). Other information service firms (accountants, advertisers and lawyers) have traditionally relied on non-electronic forms of information, but are increasingly using electronic information systems.

Secondary EISs are provided by firms primarily engaged in other activities such as manufacturing, mining or other services (e.g., health and transport). This category includes EISs which are provided within a company. It is particularly important for firms in high-technology manufacturing areas, such as electronics, automobiles and aerospace, many of which have quite sophisticated intra-firm electronic information systems linking production plants and offices throughout the world.

Primary and secondary EISs are becoming more important in Australia's domestic economy and for its international linkages. Foreign-owned transnational corporations in the primary EIS area (banking and finance) are expanding their operations in Australia; conversely Australian-based EIS transnationals are expanding internationally, especially in the Asia-Pacific region. Australia's economy is becoming increasingly reliant on international telecommunications flows underpinning trade in both primary and secondary EISs.

## AUSTRALIA'S INTERNATIONAL TELECOMMUNICATIONS TRAFFIC

In common with other industrialized countries, Australia's international telecommunications traffic has grown rapidly in recent years. A major component of this traffic growth arises from the emergence of international trade in EISs. From 1980 to 1985 the growth rate for domestic telecommunications was 8.0 per cent per annum for telephone calls.[3] In contrast, the growth rate was 35.6 per cent per annum for international telephone traffic.[4] The Overseas Telecommunications Commission (OTC) expects this growth rate to expand in the future. It estimated that it carried 1000 giga characters (giga $= 10^9$) of international information in 1984; within five years it expected to carry more than 5000 giga characters and by 1996 over 40 000.[5] However, the international telecommunications business is still a relatively small percentage of domestic telecommunications—for example, OTC's revenue was only 8.6 per cent of Telecom's in 1985.

It is difficult to disaggregate telecommunications traffic by type of user, since business and private subscribers make use of the public telephone network. However, it is recognized that the personal usage component of Australia's international telephone traffic is quite high (approximately 40 per cent), although this figure would be substantially lower were other business services (telex, data and leased line) to be included in total international telecommunications.

There are three main reasons for the growth in international business telecommunications in recent years. The growth reflects, in part, the rapid internationalization of production in some manufacturing (e.g., automobiles, electronics and computers) and primary EIS industries (e.g., banking and finance and computer services). Transnational corporations in these industries have increasingly integrated production, marketing, R & D and finance on a global basis. While demand from government and other business users for international telecommunications has grown, it has expanded particularly rapidly from these firms. For the global corporation, its international telecommunications network represents the central nervous system that allows it to respond rapidly to changes in its operating environment.

Rapid change in information technologies has been a major factor in stimulating growth of international telecommunications. New telecommunications technologies such as communications satellite systems and submarine fibre optic cables have dramatically lowered costs. The cost of overcoming distance has been greatly reduced; this has been of particular significance for Australia, which is far from its major trading partners.

A third factor influencing growth of international telecommunications is the social, economic and political environment. An issue that is provoking considerable debate internationally and in Australia has been the pressure to introduce competition in international and domestic telecommunications. Much of the thrust emanates from large international telecommunications users and from governments of major industrialized countries (US, UK and Japan) who are likely to enhance their status as international telecommunications hubs as well as attracting additional EISs.

## NATIONAL SOVEREIGNTY

National sovereignty has been defined as a country's ability to influence the direction of its political, economic, social and cultural change.[6] Another definition refers to the legal powers a state has to control national policies and to exercise jurisdiction over a specific tract of territory.[7] An important component of national sovereignty reflects the desire of a nation to protect itself and its citizens from negative outside influences. However, there is also an important positive element: the goal of developing and implementing a nation's economic, cultural and social policies.

No state has complete national sovereignty. Some have argued that the shift towards an international information economy is increasingly making national boundaries irrelevant; they argue that national institutions should adapt to the new international forces. In reality, Australia's economy reflects a balance between international, national and regional forces, and while the point of balance may be shifting towards the international end, this shift is not necessarily the inexorable force that some would have it.

National sovereignty encompasses a variety of issues. There have been fears of cultural domination expressed in the Third World and in some industrialized countries (Canada and France) over the dominance of the US in international information flows. For the Third World this issue is closely related to the more general debate which has raged since the 1960s over the free flow of information, especially in the news agency, television, film and advertising industries.[8] Another question, one which has been little examined, is whether transnational companies pose an economic threat to national sovereignty. A number of countries fear that they are becoming branch plant/office economies, controlled via sophisticated international information systems from corporation headquarters. They see new telecommunications and information technologies as further reinforcing this geographic centralization of control. However, it is by no means clear that telecommunications and other information technologies do, in fact, encourage centralization of control and decision-making. From the limited evidence available, it would appear that transnational companies have used information technology in a variety of ways. Some have decentralized their decision-making, while others have centralized it. Another approach has been to centralize corporate policy-making and long-term planning at the head office, while decentralizing production and marketing decisions so as to be more responsive to the market.

## POSSIBLE THREATS TO NATIONAL SOVEREIGNTY

Most discussion of Australia's vulnerability has been confined to the impact of economic or political embargoes on commodities such as oil and strategic minerals. Despite the fact that Australia is moving towards an information economy, we are still more comfortable in considering the impact of changes involving physical objects. But now we must consider to what extent the Australian economy could continue to operate if key sources of international information were disrupted.

Vulnerability in the international EIS area may arise because a foreign company and/or country has a monopoly in the supply of a service, and for commercial, strategic or other political reasons supply to Australian users is interrupted. Uncertainty may also arise from physical disruption to the telecommunications network (terrorist attack, natural disaster, etc.) or through criminal tampering with the network. Computer-related crime could occur at the source of the service, in the electronic transmission of the information, or at the end-user location in Australia.

This issue in international telecommunications and EISs must be seen in the context of Australia's position in the international economy. With a relatively small economy heavily reliant on international trade, it is inevitable that Australia will be vulnerable to international economic and political events. In addition, many Australian industries have a relatively high level of foreign control and are dependent on foreign-sourced technology. Thus Australia's vulnerability in the international EIS area is not so much greater than its vulnerability in other areas, especially in high-technology fields. On the other hand, whether vulnerability in information is intrinsically more significant is an issue for debate.

## Physical disruption of international information systems

One of the more easily comprehended areas of vulnerability is the physical disruption to international information systems from such causes as military or terrorist attack, natural disasters or equipment malfunction. The level of vulnerability of the economy to such events depends largely on the degree of redundancy built into computer and telecommunications systems. For example, in most cases malfunction of international telecommunications equipment or facilities could be expected to cause temporary inconvenience. Traffic generally could be directed via other routes. Interruptions to services on Intelsat's Indian or Pacific Ocean satellites or to international submarine cables linking Australia to the rest of the world would stretch capacity on the alternative services. However, OTC has built a substantial degree of redundancy into its available capacity to cater for such a contingency.

A more important cause for concern in Australia is the possibility of equipment failure in a major international financial centre. The increasing level of integration of international financial markets carries with it the requirement that key nodal points of the system (London, New York and in the future Tokyo) must be able to operate without computer or telecommunications system faults.

## Competition in international telecommunications

A country's vulnerability will also be influenced by changes in the regulatory structure governing international telecommunications. It was mentioned earlier that transnational corporations and governments of large industrialized countries (US, UK and Japan) were pressing for competition to be introduced in international telecommunications. Competition is likely to increase Australia's vulnerability. At present over 60 per cent of Australia's international telecommunications traffic is carried by Intelsat, a co-operative owned by over 100 nations. Competition from privately-owned satellite companies (there are a number of US proposals) would weaken Intelsat and is likely to lead to higher international telecommunications rates for Australian users.[9] In a fully competitive international environment, it is possible that Australia would have to rely on foreign-owned companies for vital international communications.

## Reliance on the US

Australia's reliance on US suppliers of EISs is a significant component of its vulnerability. Australian and other international users of EISs might not receive a very high priority in the restoration of services in the event of a major US natural disaster. In addition, competition in US long-distance telecommunications services might fragment the market and reduce the ability of carriers to restore services in the event of a natural disaster. There are many other possibilities. The basic problem is that vulnerability is substantially heightened if a nation relies on a single country for the supply of a service or a product, rather than on a number of countries.

One method of reducing Australia's vulnerability in this area would be for the Australian government to encourage Australian firms to buy at least some of their EISs from non-US based firms. The difficulty with this strategy is that these firms tend to have less sophisticated services. While other industrialized countries such as the UK and Japan have targeted production of EISs as a growth area, it does not seem likely that US dominance in this area will be seriously challenged in the foreseeable future.

## Extraterritorial application of national laws

This question has arisen in the international trade area following attempts by US courts to apply anti-trust laws internationally and by the US government to apply trade sanctions. While this issue may seem to be of importance only for a small group of international trade lawyers, it has quite important implications for national sovereignty.

The US has encountered strong opposition from other industrialized countries (including Australia) in attempting to apply its laws in other countries.[10] There has also been considerable debate over the US government's attempt to impose strict rules on all Western countries concerning the export of information equipment and EISs (e.g., computer software) to Communist countries. Furthermore, imposition of trade sanctions by the US government (e.g., over the Soviet gas pipeline to Western Europe) led to a fierce debate with Western European countries.

At first sight these international trade legal issues would appear to have little to do with the international information economy. We have seen earlier that the international information economy is facilitating growing interdependency amongst nations. This interdependency requires a relatively open international environment, one in which there are few barriers to international trade in EIS and international information flows. Moreover, interdependency only exists if exchanges between countries are relatively balanced. It can be contrasted with a dependency relationship—one in which linkages are unbalanced, with one or more countries dominating international trade and/or information flows.

The issue of barriers to international trade in EISs and information flows has been extensively debated in recent years. The US government has strongly supported large multinationals in their push to liberalize trade in services and introduce competition in international telecommunications. However, its position is quite contradictory: despite the US government's avowed commitment to free trade principles, its attempts to gain extraterritorial application of its national laws restrict the internationalization of industry. This is particularly true in the information equipment area (electronics and computers), but is becoming increasingly important in the EIS area.

The US government is likely to minimize the extraterritorial application of its laws, aware that it has already created a significant backlash in numerous countries (Western Europe, Australia and Canada). However, the US still has laws in place which could quickly be brought to bear. It is also likely that Australian companies or the Australian government may avoid conflict by abiding by US laws wherever they operate, thus avoiding the threat of anti-trust action or the imposition of US national security laws.

There may not be major direct conflicts between Australia and the US over these issues. It is more likely that Australian firms will be caught up as third parties in disputes between the US and other countries. This was the situation in the Santos case. An Australian company, Santos, was affected by trade sanctions when the US government imposed its Export Administration Act in the Russia to Western Europe natural gas pipeline case in 1982. Santos had to change its purchase of pipeline equipment from Dresser France to Dresser in the US when the US government ordered that the French company be disconnected from the US computer data base.

## CONCLUSION

This chapter has focused on the impact of the international information economy on Australia's national sovereignty. There seems to be little appreciation amongst policy makers of the dangers involved. Few in the community are aware of the vulnerability of the economy; nor are they aware of trends which may increase this vulnerability in the future.

Australia's linkages to the international information economy pose significant opportunities as well as dangers. The government must introduce policies which allow the country to take advantage of the opportunities emerging, especially in the Asia-Pacific region, while at the same time minimizing the risks associated with national sovereignty.

Part of the difficulty in recommending specific government policies to reaffirm national sovereignty is that we know little about how the domestic information economy operates, let alone the international one. What types of information are vital to Australia's economy? What are the key public and private organizations that must be able to receive, process and transmit information?

Banks and other financial institutions are key organizations. To what extent has international electronic funds transfer made the Australian banking system more vulnerable? For example, the crash of a major international bank in the US might cause a ripple effect which would spread virtually instantaneously to other countries. Rescue operations involving co-ordination between the US federal reserve system and other countries' reserve banks might be difficult to achieve in a short time.[11]

There are many other questions which need to be considered. What would be the effect of a strike by telecommunications unions which halted linkages between Australia and other countries? How resilient would various public and private organizations be in the face of a breakdown or natural disaster at a key computer centre?

Assuming that Australia continues to shift into an international and domestic information economy over the next decade, vulnerability (both domestic and international) is likely to rise. Are all organizations likely to be equally vulnerable? Some have decentralized decision-making and computer processing down to the local level and thus reduced their reliance on international information sources or even head offices within Australia. Others are likely to be more vulnerable.

Australian society has not in the past considered these types of forward planning issues. Planners have tended to react to specific problems *ad hoc*. Unfortunately, this strategy is unlikely to be successful in tomorrow's highly interconnected information economy.

# CHAPTER 12

# NEW TECHNOLOGY AND INTERNATIONAL PRIVACY ISSUES*

## Michael Kirby

## THE NEW 'MARXISM'

The other day, as light relief to Archbold's *Criminal Pleadings* and Dicey's *Law of the Constitution*, I was reading the writings of Marx. Not, mind you, Karl, but Garry Marx, a New York academic. Asserting that popular culture, and hit tunes, can sometimes convey, even subliminally, important political and social messages, Marx took as an illustration the hit song of the pop group The Police. Hidden away in the words, he said, was a timely warning to the younger generation of the dangers of the new information technology. The song is 'Every Breath You Take'. Here it is with Marx's analysis:

Every breath you take [breath analyser]

Every move you make [motion detector]

Every bond you break [polygraph-lie detector]

Every step you take [electronic anklet]

Every single day [continuous monitoring]

Every word you say [bugs, wire taps, mikes]

Every night you stay [light amplifier]

Every vow you break [voice stress analysis]

Every claim you stake [computer matching]

Every smile you fake [brain wave analysis]

I'll be watching you [video surveillance].

Marx's thesis is as frightening as it is simple. We stand at the brink of remarkable developments in the thriving new technology of informatics both in the public and private sectors. Some of the developments are regulated by current law. Many of them are outside. Computers may match the hundreds of profiles built up on all of us. In the last

---

* This chapter is the text of a speech delivered at a forum on access to information and privacy, Ottawa, 6 March 1986.

decade, there has been a massive increase in the ability to collect and process intrusive information about all of us which, but a few years ago, would have been regarded as utterly private and totally inaccessible—even to the most powerful government official or corporate enterprise.[1] Satellites can spot a car or person from 9000 metres up. They have been used for surveillance of drug traffickers. Light amplifiers, developed for the Vietnam war, can be used with a variety of cameras and binoculars to intrude into the private moment. National security agencies monitor hundreds of telephones. The Hong Kong government is testing an electronic system for monitoring where, when and how fast a car is driven. A small radio receiver in the car picks up low-frequency signals from wire loops set into the street. It then transmits back to a central authority the car's identification number. The system was proposed as an efficient means for the relatively innocent task of checking the payment of road tax in the congested traffic areas of Victoria Island. But what a boon it provides, or would provide, for continuous monitoring and surveillance.

This is not alarmist talk. The features of the new information technology which endanger the value of individual privacy are now well known. According to Marx, the dangers derive from the following features of the technology in particular:

- it transcends distance, darkness and physical barriers;
- it transcends time, because of the capacity to collect and store massive amounts of data which can be retrieved whenever needed;
- it is capital- rather than labour-intensive, because it is no longer necessary to have human intervention—the computer can analyse all;
- it is universal in its application, decentralized and triggers self-activating policing;
- it has low visibility or even total invisibility;
- it grows ever more extensive and covers larger areas of life ever more deeply.

These are trite statements about a pervasive technology which is overwhelmingly beneficial in its potential to release mankind from the millstones of routine and mindless drudgery. However, a poll conducted in 1985 by Louis Harris-France in eight industrial countries indicates that 'invasion of privacy and unemployment continue to be viewed as two significant consequences of data processing'.[2] In the United States, 68 per cent of those polled agreed that it would be increasingly possible to use computer data banks to infringe personal privacy. Knowledgeable people who are not Luddites recognize that a hitherto important feature of our form of societies is seriously endangered by what is otherwise a beneficial technological development. Moreover, it is a development which has distinctly positive features for the enhancement of freedom. For example, the new information technology promises improvement in cost-effective access to official information. In this way the public accountability of politicians and bureaucrats may be extended far beyond the occasional visit to the ballot box which was previously the theoretical occasion for enforcing the ultimate accountability of the executive government to the people.

In Western democracies three changes have occurred which promote the demand for privacy and freedom of information (FOI) laws.

1 The significant growth in the role of the public sector, precipitated by the urgent needs of the Second World War and continued and expanded ever since to create a vast panoply of agencies and officialdom, demolished many of the vestiges of the mythology of ministerial accountability. It has led to a rational insistence upon new institutions and rights which translate theoretical accountability into daily practice.[3]

2 The general advance in the education of the community has had a dual impact. It has created an ever-expanding pool of well-informed citizens, impatient with the paternalistic notion that administrators necessarily know best. It has also created, particularly in the educated middle class, a group of people willing to utilize new rights and to enforce them in the courts and in the protective administrative agencies set up.

3 The new technology itself, as Marx and others have demonstrated, presented novel problems, including problems of data protection and data security; but it also presented potential solutions. Keys, passwords and encriptions could be introduced to bar access to personal information, even to an inquisitive civil servant who, in the old days, might have had access to paper files. On-line facilities can assure the data subject, potentially, a right of access to data about himself or herself, in a way that the inefficiency of the old systems could not necessarily ensure.

Thus, the issue in a nutshell is one of thinking, as the Americans say, 'positive', taking advantage of the remarkable and increasingly pervasive technology of informatics whilst, at the same time, acting with resolution to defend elements of individual privacy deemed important for the liberty of mankind in the future.

## THE THREAD OF ARIADNE

The past decade or so has seen important legislative responses to informatics in all the advanced English-speaking democracies. Freedom of information and privacy laws have been enacted in the United States and Canada.[4] Privacy legislation has been enacted in the United Kingdom. But, although 57 per cent of the British people in 1985 told an opinion poll that they thought FOI would help protection of rights 'a great deal',[5] the United Kingdom government seems to adhere to the old mythology of ministerial accountability, the Official Secrets Act and the world of 'leaks' which tends to accompany, nowadays, regimes of too much secrecy. The Ponting trial[6] and the Westland helicopter affair all show what happens in secretive administrations in the age of the photocopier.

New Zealand has enacted an FOI law,[7] indeed has been looking at reform of that law and at the enactment of privacy legislation.[8] In Australia, a Freedom of Information Act was enacted by Federal parliament in 1982. It contained an important section for rights of access to personal information and for the protection of private information. Comprehensive Federal privacy laws have been promised.[9] But hand in hand with these developments comes a proposal for a national identity card to co-ordinate Federal data banks as a suggested means of combating tax and social security fraud.[10]

Recently, I had to offer a foreword to a forthcoming publication, to be printed in Canada, on the problems and prospects of these information laws.[11] Looking through the reports of Ms Inger Hansen and Dr Harold Relyea, and the report on the Australian legislation offered by Senator Alan Missen, it became clear that a number of common themes were emerging. They chart the way ahead for those concerned about information law in the last decade of the twentieth century. To some extent, the themes are similar. With differing emphasis, the authors call attention to concerns which will clearly affect the law and administrative practices involved in the exercise of privacy and FOI rights for years to come.

Hansen and Relyea stress the concern in Canada and the United States that FOI is being used (or abused) to breach the legitimate expectations of business confidentiality. This confidentiality may sometimes be undermined by the revelation, pursuant to FOI law, of information supplied by business (usually under compulsion) to the government. How are these competing rights to be reconciled and the integrity of FOI maintained, whilst ensuring legitimate claims to business secrecy and candid supply of business data to government?

Concern is also expressed in Canada and the United States about the use of FOI to undermine, frustrate and delay the processes of law enforcement. Particular anxiety is felt about the so-called 'mosaic' phenomenon—as a result of which, even where identifiers have been deleted, some material supplied pursuant to FOI can assist anti-social persons to identify public informers or to secure other information which public policy suggests should be kept secret.

Concern about the cost of FOI is a theme running through all reports on the operation of information legislation. There is the suggestion that this is a luxury which, however desirable in principle, our communities simply cannot afford. There is also the suggestion that, depending as it does on the activities of enthusiastic individuals, our FOI and privacy laws are very much the guardians of the educated middle class. They provide little in the way of enhanced freedom for those people who are most dependent on, and under the surveillance of, government—the social security recipients, veterans, hospital patients and others whose very position of dependence often makes the enforcement of their information right a matter of theory rather than practice.

In Australia the concern about FOI and privacy laws has changed in the last decade. From the early debates about the numerous exemptions and conclusive ministerial certificates under the FOI Act, the concern today has shifted. So few ministerial exemptions have been claimed that the battleground has moved. Now, the counter-reformation comes from the bureaucrats who point repeatedly to the cumbersome and costly machinery to which they must devote scarce resources. And those concerned about spreading the impact of FOI and privacy access rights point to the narrow usage of those rights, the widespread ignorance about them, their substantial confinement to the educated middle class and the retreat from earlier public campaigns to promote general knowledge by media advertising, pamphlets and the like.[12]

At this level of the debate it would be possible to trace a thread of Ariadne through the controversies. Common themes undoubtedly exist. There is some evidence of a counter-reformation, as attention is laid by bureaucrats and politicians in many lands upon cost and the various problems which the first decade of information legislation has disclosed.

Instead of taking this course, I have decided, with due modesty, to propound the ten information commandments. It was said of President Wilson's fourteen points that he had divined four more than the Almighty. Being a more diffident type I prefer to follow the Mosaic tradition.

## THE TEN INFORMATION COMMANDMENTS

### 1 *Contemporary technological developments endanger human rights and civil liberties and require responses from society—including the legal system.*

This first 'commandment' states the obvious. It is not confined to informatics. The most remarkable feature of the late twentieth century is the coincidence, at one moment of history, of three important technological developments. I refer to nuclear fission, bio-technology and informatics. Each of these developments has implications for human rights and civic freedoms. Information technology presents problems, some of which have been identified already by Garry Marx. Bio-technology presents quandaries which go to the very definition of human life itself. Human cloning, in-vitro fertilization, the growing of human body parts and numerous other features of genetic engineering and bio-technology present major dilemmas to the philosopher, the lawyer and the law-maker. In the Australian Parliament, at the time of writing, a parliamentary committee is examining a private member's Bill designed to restrict and control many bio-tech. developments, in

some of which Australian scientists have made notable contribu-
tions.[13] Of nuclear fission, I need say nothing—except that, unless the
international community can bring this technology under effective
international control, the long-run prospects of mankind's surviving
accidents, mistake or nuclear folly appear problematical. So the starting point—the beginning of wisdom—is a realization of the enormous
challenge which technology presents to humanity in our generation.
We need a Luther of jurisprudence to lead us to the legal solutions and
political leaders of wisdom to lead our communities thoughtfully to
the responses that preserve life and freedom.

## 2 The fertile common law system, even as enhanced in some countries by constitutional rights, is insufficient to provide adequate responses to the challenges of technology. More legislation is needed.

There are some people who say that the common law, developed by
the judges, will be adequate to defend our liberties—in the future as it
has in the past. No doubt there is a role for the common law. It must
surely respond to technological change. Benjamin Cardozo once said
that the law, like the traveller, must prepare for the morrow. In the
United States, with the famous language of the Bill of Rights, and lately
in Canada with the Charter of Rights and Freedoms, a scope is offered
to the judiciary to enhance the creative element which has always
existed in the common law. But even in such countries, and still more
so in countries such as Australia, without such a catalyst for judicial
creativity in the protection of rights in the modern era, more will be
needed. Recently the High Court of Australia reversed a decision in
which I had participated. It was a decision relevant to information
rights. The Court of Appeal had declared that, in modern circumstances, the common law of natural justice required the giving of
reasons by public officials enjoying legislative discretions.[14] The High
Court, referring to old authorities, many of them preceding the three
developments to which I have referred, unanimously ruled that a right
to reasons was not required by the rules of natural justice.[15] Development of the law here, it was said, was for the parliament, not the
courts. A signal was sent out cautioning against judicial creativity. It
was said that in other countries of the common law, for example India,
where a right to reasons is now established, constitutional considerations, in the form of fundamental rights, might explain and justify
developments in the law. Perhaps in Canada the law will respond
more readily to changing times and changing technology because of
the facility provided by the Charter of Rights and Freedoms. But in
Australia, as in New Zealand, England and elsewhere, the judiciary
since the nineteenth century and the reforms of parliament has, with
notable exceptions, preferred to emphasize the non-creative features
of the common law. Yet a signal that calls for judicial restraint calls

equally for legislative attention, in default of which the judges will be urged to remedy wrongs and to provide defences to freedom.

### 3 In some cases, the technology itself demands or even produces legal reform.

This third rule refers to the tendency of modern technology to undermine current law or to render it irrelevant or ineffective. I have already mentioned the way in which the photocopier undermines excessive secrecy. Doubtless this is why photocopiers are kept under lock and key in the Soviet Union. The technology of photographic reproduction and on-line linkages reduces the capacity to keep things secret. The self-same technology that presents problems of privacy promotes a flow of information that tends to enhance accountability both in the public and private sectors. But in the field of informatics, the results can be surprising. One case is well known and is called to attention by Professor Jon Bing of Norway. A social scientist in Norway sought on-line access, under United States FOI law, to information on Nato deployments in Norway. Such information was a state secret under Norwegian law, and the social scientist was prosecuted in Norway.[16] Information technology, with its international applications, could undermine the effective operation of the sovereign laws of domestic jurisdiction.

### 4 The people are not always the best judges of their own interests. Informed observers have a duty to identify dangers to freedom.

One of the chief arguments which the Cabinet minister proposing a computerized national identity card in Australia continually refers to is that public opinion polls show that nearly 70 per cent of Australians favour a national identity card with photograph.[17] In a democracy, it is natural for intellectuals to bow to the corporate wisdom of the people. If the people want an ID card, why should they be denied such a facility, especially if it would help combat welfare and tax fraud? The answer, sadly, is that the public is all too often willing to participate in the destruction or erosion of its own liberties. It is to informed people (particularly lawyers conscious of our long constitutional history and the famous struggles for freedom), that there falls the sometimes unpopular function of holding out against the popular tide. Opinion polls may persistently favour the reintroduction of the death penalty. They may favour the return of flogging and, who knows, even transportation to a far-off place, such as Australia. But such opinions may be based upon false impressions or ignorance of the available data. They may ignore the statistics that show the ineffectiveness of such punishments. They may ignore the statistics that show the fall in jury convictions where capital punishment is available. They may be based on ignorance of the countervailing effects of such punishments. So it may be with a national identity card. It may be based on a desire of people without access to gold American Express cards to have a nice plastic card such as other people have. It might be based on the notion that 'if you have nothing to hide', the card can do no harm. It might conjure up the memory of the occasion when proof of identity would have been useful. But it remains for those who are aware of the special relationship that exists in countries of the common law between authority and the citizen to point to the dangers. A dentist who survived Auschwitz may declare that the best thing about living in Australia (it could equally be Canada, the United States or England) is that he is never liable to be stopped on the corner by someone in uniform with the demand '*Papiere!*'. Yet provide a universal computerized ID card and the risk exists that the data base will be enhanced and that more and more officials will seek access to it, in the name of efficiency—and that in due course carrying the card will be obligatory. Then producing it will become a commonplace and, ultimately (in response, no doubt, to some outrage) obligatory. In the space of a few years, an important principle that marks off the intrusion of officialdom into our lives could be quite easily demolished. And the intrusion might not just be physical. It might go on behind the scenes—as intrusion into the data profile where more and more decisions affecting the subject may be made without the slightest knowledge of the data subject.

Lulled by a trivializing diet of soap operas, cowboy Westerns and Manhattan gun battles, our people become indifferent spectators to or even conspirators in the erosion of their own freedoms. Should we care? Should we who are aware of the long battles for freedom also surrender, acknowledging that some erosion of privacy is inevitable as a product of the new information technology? My Fourth Commandment says that we *should* care. It is the responsibility of politicians, and those who advise them, to work, even in the face of popular indifference or opposition, for the preservation of hard-won freedoms. For once they are lost they are rarely regained.

## 5 The costs of information rights must be counted; but so must the intangible benefits.

In the jargon of the economist, it is important for lawyers who talk of liberty and freedom to take into account the incremental costs involved in the externalities to decision-making. The protection of freedom and the assurance of fairness certainly have a cost. It involves the assignment of scarce resources. The recent *Singh* decision in Canada, obliging hearings for refugee immigrants, was a step towards administrative fairness. But clearly the cost of providing this facility will run into millions of dollars. The provision of the facility to the persons affected will necessarily result in the denial of benefits to others. That is nothing more than the simple consequence of the economic problem.[18] So it is in information rights. There is now a great deal of talk, particularly in Australia, concerning the costs of FOI and privacy rights. There is a similar debate in the United States. But whereas the American FOI legislation is now a robust adolescent, the same cannot be said of the equivalent laws in Canada, Australia and New Zealand. The combination of talk about cost of the provision of information rights, the inevitable concern by politicians about skeletons they would rather leave in the computer cupboard, and the hankering of not a few public servants for a return to the 'good old days', all present the danger of the information counter-Reformation. It is a danger which supporters of information rights must repel. They must work with special vigour in countries such as Canada and Australia because of the relative ease with which governments, dominating the legislature, could secure the rolling back of legislative entitlements to information—whether public or personal. The rolling back of such rights can be done by frank legislative amendment and repeal. But it can also be done, in practice, by the introduction of or increase in charges. These may effectively bar some of the more deserving people from exercising their rights. Or it can be done by cutting back publicity about the existence of the rights, so that they remain (in practice) the province of the media, of corporations and of educated middle-class citizens. It is natural that in more difficult economic times governments should be concerned about the costs of information rights. The direct costs include not only the administrative staffs and bureaucratic time. To them must be added the provision of court rooms, judges and tribunal members, shorthand writers and so on. As well, there are the opportunity costs—the other facilities and benefits foregone by virtue of the decision to stay with information rights.

These concerns have led government ministers[19] and the leader of the opposition[20] in Australia to foreshadow the possible winding back or limitation of review mechanisms for the enforcement of information rights. This is sure to be an important issue in the decade ahead. It may be that corporations and others who are major users of such rights should pay a differential fee in recognition of the fact that they can pass such business expenses on to consumers using their products. It may also be that attention needs to be given to the more cost-effective way of delivering information: avoiding the cumbersome, expensive and dilatory machinery of courts and tribunals. But when the public costs are added up, so must be the public benefits. And the relativities must be considered. They include the well-known statistic that the cost of FOI in the United States is less than the upkeep of lawns on golf courses for overseas defence personnel. And as Dr Relyea points out, against the cost of providing information that people want to know must be considered the cost of official government information services that nowadays pour out thinly disguised propaganda, repeated through media handouts, concerning what the government *wants* people to know. The former may be a healthy corrective, on occasion, to the latter.

## 6 *Information laws must be developed flexibly because of changing technology and the rapidly changing perceptions of the problems.*

Not to devise and implement adequate privacy laws, in the inadequacy of the common law and current legislation, is to make a decision. It is to stand quietly by whilst the technology itself erodes hitherto valued rights. But the counterpart of this principle is that inflexible laws can hinder resolution of the problem they have been introduced to solve. Many of the laws already put in place rely heavily on the right of individual access as a means of protecting individual privacy rights. But the effective utilization of this most beneficial right depends upon large assumptions. It depends upon knowledge by the individual that there is something to be concerned about. Yet if there is no notification that you are in the system, decisions may be made that are vital to your life while you may be blissfully ignorant. Similarly, the right of access makes large assumptions about individual initiative and enthusiasm.

In fact, apathy, resignation or a feeling of powerlessness may necessitate other solutions, if true data protection is to be afforded to people other than the powerful and articulate who exert their rights. There is a tendency in our kind of society to slip into legislative mythology. It is an easy and convenient myth to believe that accountability is provided by a right of access and that information rights are thereby protected. In fact such facilities should be seen as the start of a long journey—not arrival in the Promised Land.

## 7 *Information rights must extend from the public sector (where they have been developed) to the private sector.*

So far, comprehensive information laws have concentrated on the public sector. This is natural, for it is in that sector that critical information affecting all citizens exists. But increasingly important in our lives, and often insusceptible to national control, are large corporations—including transnational corporations. People in the private sector tend to be foremost in asserting the right of accountability by public officials and access to public data; but the self-same principle has relevance to the private sector as well. Its full relevance has yet to be worked out.

Of course, there is already much accountability by the private sector, including in the market. But information rights concern individual power, and power exerted in dealings with the corporate state may be equally necessary in dealings with private enterprise. Voluntary guidelines, such as compliance with the OECD privacy principles, may provide a starting point, but it is scarcely likely that this will be adequate in the long term.

## 8 *Information technology presents international issues that require international solutions.*

The need for transborder solutions to information rights is self-evident in federations such as Australia, Canada and the United States. But there is a wider international stage. The technology itself is virtually universal, and the problems presented necessarily transcend state borders. The OECD guidelines were developed in the hope of stimulating consistency in legislative and administrative approaches to information rights in the context of privacy. Now, other international agencies are endeavouring to develop rules which can facilitate common approaches. UNESCO has just embarked on a major informatics programme. The Intergovernmental Bureau for Informatics in Rome has established a commission to promote a dialogue on data law and policy between the advanced countries of the OECD and the developing world. The technology must interface. Gross inefficiency will result if legal regulations are incompatible and yet must be complied with by transborder flows of data. Data havens may destroy the effectiveness of information rights. The three major technological developments of our time—nuclear fission, bio-technology and informatics—require of us that we should lift our sights from parochial and purely nationalistic approaches to the law. Until now, law has been very much jurisdiction-bound, but international technology imposes on us the need for international approaches to legal regulations. We in the developed world must become more conscious of the needs and concerns of those less rich, for they follow the caravan of the information economy.

## 9 *Legal responses to information rights must attend to real problems and not content themselves with myths and mere symbols.*

This principle has already been foreshadowed. The easy thing for lawmakers to do is to establish a bureaucracy with attractive titles, set up with a fanfare announcing that information is free and privacy is henceforth guaranteed. But what is important is the fine print. It has always seemed to me that the value of the OECD guidelines lay chiefly in the formulation of a short list of relatively simple principles for information practices. If these became well known and generally accepted as a Bible of fair information practices, much would be achieved. Sanctions and advisory mechanisms are needed to deal with the problems that arise. But most people at the workface simply require a series of simple rules, ultimately backed up by the law. The simpler the rules are kept and the fewer in number, the more likely it is that fair practices will result. In the field of FOI, rights of access will not promote effective accountability unless they are reinforced by community rights of access to the public media. The concentration of the media in few hands may undermine the effectiveness of official information laws if they prevent vital information flowing through to the community at large. Thus it is the reality of information rights that we should be concerned with, not the mythology. Laws which talk of 'the consent of the data subject', for example, sound fine. But in the case of an unemployed pensioner seeking a social security benefit, or a hospital patient seeking treatment, or an employee seeking information and conscious of the risk of dismissal or reduced prospects for advancement that might follow, it may sometimes be necessary to go beyond reliance on the courageous individual. Information laws which depend exclusively on individual motivation for enforcement are much better than nothing; they are a step in the right direction, but they fall a long way short of providing effective protections against all the implications of the new technology.

## 10 *Democratic values must be preserved, and it is at least questionable whether our democratic institutions can adequately respond to the challenges of technology.*

This brings me to my last 'commandment'. I approach my conclusion on a sombre note. Those who look at the history of parliamentary democracies this century, at least in Western countries, may be generally optimistic about the future. Despite many challenges, the institutions have survived. The alternative systems are infinitely less flexible and uniformly more oppressive. But the problem for parliamentary institutions, posed by rapid technological change, is the problem of keeping pace. If nothing is done, a decision is made. Yet the very technicality of the changes makes it difficult for the lay politician (and indeed those advising him or her) to comprehend all the ramifications. Furthermore, many of the changes are highly controversial, as debates about the privacy of children against their parents and debates about bio-technology experiments clearly demonstrate. In the face of such complexity and controversy, there is a natural tendency to parliamentary inaction. It is understandable; but it is dangerous. It is especially dangerous if it coincides with the disinclination of the judges (themselves often scientifically illiterate) to mobilize the creative machinery of the common law. There are at least some signs that this is what is occurring. It is most likely to occur if the executive, which dominates parliament, loses enthusiasm for information rights. That loss of enthusiasm may be dressed up in the name of economy and cost/benefit analysis. But it may simply disguise age-old issues of power: where power is to lie. In Australia, there is much evidence of the institutional incapacity to respond. Only one State, Victoria, has enacted an FOI law. In others it is repeatedly promised, but nothing comes of the promises. Only one State, New South Wales, has a general privacy law, and that of limited effectiveness. The Federal privacy law is a long time coming. And there is much more vigour in pressing on with a national identity card, despite the dangers it poses for privacy, than in embracing privacy protection laws, limited as they may be.

In the field of information rights, public lethargy now conspires with unsympathetic noises both from government and opposition quarters.

## CONCLUSIONS

What is the result of this analysis? Is it that late twentieth century men and women of the global village, lulled into an intellectual haze by a constant diet of media trivia, have lost concern about real political accountability? Or are they indifferent to (and do they even conspire in the destruction of) privacy rights? Political accountability becomes little more than a three-yearly television war between competing electoral jingles—with political parties sold like soap powder to a people programmed to watch personality politics, devoid of concern with the large issues and obsessed by the parochial.

You might say that if 70 per cent of the people want the introduction of a facility used in other times and other places to destroy liberty, then governments and politicians must bow to the superior wisdom of the people and their assessment of their information rights.

But that wisdom ultimately depends on knowledge. And it is up to those who have the knowledge and can see the problems to act responsibly and courageously. I remain incurably optimistic. In the darker moments of contemplation, however, there is a lingering doubt. Of even greater concern than the survival of political accountability and the persistence of privacy in the age of informatics is the institutional question. In such a time of rapid change, of complex science and of high controversy, can our law-making institutions cope? That is the question that transcends even privacy and freedom of information issues. They are in a sense a microcosm of a larger problem, for if our parliamentary democracies falter here, they admit their incompetence to govern us in the twenty-first century—whose watchword and engine will be science. Accordingly, we must remain optimistic about our capacity to adapt our institutions and laws to rapid technological change. A loss of confidence or heart—and a breach of the Commandment of optimism—is a surrender to the nagging doubt that technology is inherently élitist and autocratic and that democracy, with all its inefficiencies, cannot survive into the next century. We must make it our business to ensure that this prophecy of gloom proves wrong. But the responsibility for rational optimism is ours.

*PART V*

# National Directions

# CHAPTER 13

# WHOSE REVOLUTION?

Trevor Barr

We are living, we are so often told, through a communications revolution. Many discussions of the nature of this revolution are merely technical in character, and the political and social implications of this technical revolution are often underplayed. That is, we hear much about the means of delivering information—such as by satellite, cable, microwave or fibre optics—but rarely do we see major debates about what is being delivered, by whom and why.

There appears to be limited perception in the broader community of the overall economic significance of the communications and information industries, and of their substantial prospects for economic growth. The past decade has witnessed staggering growth of the service industries in Australia's communications sector, especially in commercial television, but also for Telecom and the Overseas Telecommunications Commission.[1] According to the Scott Little report, *Information Technology in Australia*, the market for information technology and related products in Australia is expected to expand from $3.2 billion in 1982 to $7.1 billion in 1992.[2] Information industries, as a whole, have become the most significant investment area within the Australian economy. (Telecom, for instance, now spends more than $2 billion in capital works annually.) Capital works investments in the information sector as a whole (including computer network building), together with multiplier effects, could generate collective investments of the order of $25–35 billion in the next five years. The boom in the 1980s has not been in mining, oil and gas, as predicted, but in the communications and information industries. Information is the commodity of the future.

Whilst Australia, like most developed economies in the past decade, has experienced a shift towards an information-based economy, there are some major political paradoxes within this. First, a community which encourages a whole new range of electronic systems and processes referred to as information technology, also abounds with ignorance, suspicion and fear of technological change. Second, we emphasize economic development policies for the media, telecommunications and information technology industries, but tend to regard the agenda of related social concerns as 'secondary' in policy formulation. The information society has generated concerns about personal autonomy, equity and access to information, misuse of information and threats to privacy, as well as the emergence of new occupational health problems. Third, though Australia can be credited with considerable scientific innovation, and Australian industry has long been enterprising in many ways, the fact is that we can call few of the new technologies our own. The equipment or hardware associated with the information revolution has been largely imported from transnational corporations. This is not to attack the big brand names of American and Japanese corporations; it is part of a wider recognition that our status as a technological client state is a major structural economic problem for Australia. We have one of the highest deficits in trade in telecommunications and computer equipment amongst OECD countries.[3]

More widely, of course, Barry Jones keeps on reminding us that Australia's exports of technological products per head of population are now lower than those of nearly every OECD country, except for Iceland! So while information hardware has become big business in Australia, the benefits have not been gained by indigenous manufacturers, but by transnational corporations. In a manufacturing context, a short answer to the question 'whose revolution?' is the world's successful transnational corporations.

In the spheres of information and cultural products, a shift towards largely national and international markets is under way. In Australia, the political mood is changing towards the elevation of a private, corporate, deregulated information economy. There are increasing challenges, for example, to the notion of *public* institutions as worthwhile models for telecommunications and broadcasting. The same push is evident overseas, notably in the sale of British Telecom under the Thatcher administration. Internationally, broadcasting is swept up in a tide of deregulation, with the introduction of new technologies increasingly subjected only to the rules of the marketplace. New broadcasting distribution systems, such as video cassette recorders or direct broadcasting satellites, are essentially controlled by international market forces. Meanwhile, established national public broadcasting organizations, such as the BBC and the ABC, struggle to maintain their share of diminishing public resources and face pressures to diversify their funding base.

These macro-institutional trends in the information field beg many questions for policy-makers. Information policy decisions, at many levels, are now much swayed by the political climate during a period of prolonged economic recession. There is a general political shift in favour of the primacy of the marketplace, and in favour of those who can afford high-cost specialized information services. For example, news agencies such as AAP or Reuters tend to use the new technologies to commoditize information into specialized, expensive information packages.[4] More widely, some library services are moving towards the select use of proprietary data bases on a 'user pays' basis. What may be compromised in the long run is the principle of open and free access to a wide range of information in public libraries.

## INFORMATION POLICY: SCENARIOS FOR THE FUTURE

What are the broad policy alternatives for Australia's development as an information society? What are the choices, challenges and opportunities for Australia in managing its technological options for the future? Could Australia ever become a leader, or player of some significance, in the next technology stakes? Does it matter if we don't substantially develop our technological base? Are we destined to remain technologically underdeveloped and essentially a client state for other countries? How can the policy-making process ensure that the information revolution serves the widest community interest? Who will make the decisions about Australia's technological future, and how?

Four policy models are offered as food for thought.

### Scenario one: Australia is capable only of limited national technological achievement and ought to continue its reliance on traditional sources of wealth

There are several variations of this scenario. One major line of argument is that only countries such as the USA, Japan and some European countries, who have now reached an extraordinarily high level of technology sophistication, can successfully remain in the international big league. How, argue some, could Australia with its mere 16 million people possibly ever emulate what has been happening in high technology in the USA and Japan, especially given our lack of any strong tradition of successful commercialization of technological products? How, ask members of this school, can we now begin to put in place a high-technology infrastructure in a country which lacks a political process for long-term strategic planning, technological or otherwise? What we ought to do then, so the argument goes, is acknowledge that Australia will never achieve much in terms of high technology, and turn our attention instead to maximizing our strengths in existing productive areas.

The international journal *Nature* argued a version of this scenario in its July 1985 editorial 'Science at a Very Great Distance'.[5] It argued that the Hawke government had the laudable ambition of turning Australia into a technological community, but was 'in danger of talking itself into a muddle about science and technology'. It pointed to the contradiction between, on the one hand, the government's desire that technology should be made economically more valuable, and on the other, its reluctance to pursue that goal by funding research, industrial innovation and training to ensure a supply of highly skilled people from Australian tertiary institutions. *Nature* was critical of proposed economic strategies in which Australia appeared to be turning its back on its traditional sources of wealth. The government's motto, it argued, seemed to be: 'If people don't want our beef, we'll do research on something else'. The new areas spelled out by government for special development treatment—bio-technology, information, robotics and the application of computer-aided design to manufacturing technology and materials—were regarded as problematic in terms of their possible international success. *Nature* argued that Australia with 16 million people 'cannot be (and does not need to be) a powerful source of innovation and production across the whole field which it now wishes to explore'.

Advocates of this scenario tend to divorce technology policy from major economic problems and trends. The *Nature* editorial observed that Australia ships metal ores and the coals with which to reduce them to countries overseas. Why, then, did we not build a major industrial base around such natural advantages, but choose instead to ship raw materials to countries such as Japan, who gained the manufacturing benefits? Australia's medicine has the highest reputation internationally, yet as *Nature* then asks 'where are the pharmaceutical industries that would have sprung up elsewhere?'. Having identified these structural economic problems though, the *Nature* editorial appears resignedly to accept that Australia could never reform such underlying economic inadequacies. They meekly say that 'there is no harm in offering people incentives to see their bright ideas turned into saleable products' but regard as 'absurd' pressure from government 'to ensure that Australian innovations are exploited only by Australian companies'. Their call is for Australia to build more energetically on the strengths it already has in scientific endeavour, and for future development to be in areas such as the application of bio-technology in agriculture. For *Nature*, the Australian government ought to 'meddle less' and patiently accept that Australia will not have a technological revolution overnight.

A more radical version of this scenario challenges any 'drive towards growth' model. This would argue that we need to accept that the level of economic development of a nation is tied to its technological capacity, but that Australia should not embrace high-technology development policies which are doomed to fail, or which are undesirable anyway. The corollary is national acceptance of lower standards of living than have been the norm for Australia, and a fundamental community reassessment of economic values, work and lifestyle. The notion that we accept and adjust ourselves to being a nation of technological drop-outs in the future is rarely debated, and remains politically unacceptable in the late 1980s.

Arguments in favour of this first scenario are usually refuted on economic grounds. Our existing economic base is vulnerable, with agricultural and mining products dependent on the vagaries of world market prices. How, argue the economic rationalists, can we possibly

divorce ourselves from international economic trends? So, if information is the commodity of the future, we must 'run' with it.

## Scenario two: Australia opts for a fundamental change of development policy towards establishment of highly privatized, deregulated communications industries

Protagonists of this school of thought put the case for privatization and
deregulation across the whole economic spectrum, including the
information technology, telecommunications and media industries.
They favour the transfer of ownership and control of public enterprises to the private sector wherever possible, and an environment
where many private companies can try out innovations and succeed or
fail according to market demands. Privatization has become a slogan
for change and an experimental strategy for recovery in several countries, with a great deal of attention focused on the gamble by Britain's
Conservative government. Under Margaret Thatcher, the British government has embarked on major sell-offs of former public enterprises
in oil, gas, transport and aerospace industries, as well as a share market
offer for British Telecom.

The privatization case is generally stated in extremely broad terms,
with a set of assertions that often amount to little more than hunches or
beliefs. The targets for privatization are inevitably selective, concentrating on those public-sector components that will obviously
generate good returns for their new owners, or on those with predicted
long-term growth prospects. The rhetoric of the debate is fascinating.
Consider, for instance, these remarks by a leading protagonist for privatization in the United Kingdom, Masden Pirie, appropriately the
President of the Adam Smith Institute in London:

> Sometimes I recall a typical day in Britain in 1979. Getting up in the morning to the
> sounds of the state radio, and, with my British Steel spoon, cutting into my Mar-
> keting Board egg and heading out in the British Leyland car, pausing to say hello to
> the state postman and maybe the local state garbage collector as he dropped rubbish
> into the street, dropping the children off at the state school, dropping the wife off at
> the state health centre and maybe phoning the state travel agent to book a trip, on
> the state airline, or on the state railways.[6]

For Pirie 'the public sector is always heavily overmanned' and Britain
had 'an incredibly big government deficit' in 1979. He adds that though
Mrs Thatcher was credited with victory over Argentinian General
Galtiere, 'her real victory has been over the public sector of the British
economy'. According to Pirie, despite staggering levels of unemployment, everyone benefits from privatization.

The privatization lobby plays upon assumptions that public enterprises are somehow inherently inefficient, costly or overstaffed, and
incapable of initiating or managing successful entrepreneurial ventures. They assert that the private sector by comparison is efficient,
cost-effective and innovative. Unfortunately, debates about privatization are often conducted in terms of such untested propositions or a set

of polarized cliches. The central argument about the virtues of privatization and deregulation involves the validity of the claim that the consequent increase in competition will lead to national economic growth. In the Australian telecommunications industry a collective of major private-sector operators proposed in the late 1970s that Telecom ownership be divided into Telecom Basic and Telecom Enhanced, which would have opened up the existing statutory corporation to greater private-sector competition, at a price. Business Telecommunications Services argued that 'an increased level of private participation in telecommunications services is required if the demands of customers are to be satisfied, and Australia as a nation is to benefit from new technologies and service opportunities'.[7] Similarly, economists of the privatization school, such as Trengove, have argued that government interference in Australian telecommunications markets through Telecom's legislated monopoly was 'designed to transfer income and wealth between market participants' and that 'economic barriers to entry have lowered the potential benefits from competitive action'.[8] The UK will provide the litmus test for such claims.

Though the drive towards privatization is most intense in telecommunications, institutions which construct and distribute cultural products are also undergoing comparable change. In broadcasting, for instance, public-service broadcasting organizations face economic pressures, and there is support for dismemberment of the public service as the preferred model for the allocation of cultural resources. In Australia, prophets of privatization have put the Australian Broadcasting Corporation under intense attack in recent years and also advocated the closure of our multicultural broadcasting organization, the Special Broadcasting Service.[9] There are signs, too, that the introduction of new technologies to Australia associated with broadcasting, such as cable television, would most likely be the exclusive province of private-sector participants.[10]

Proponents of privatization argue the general propositions that increased competition promotes widespread economic benefit, that deregulation means a desirable reduction in government involvement, and that the sale of public assets, or reduction of public appropriation, will also reduce government deficits. They also hold the general view that when it comes to the introduction of new technologies then a 'let it rip' strategy for the private sector is more desirable than any planned implementation of change. But surely in a more freewheeling Australian economy multinational corporations will exert a stranglehold on new markets in electronic technology and information goods and services? Surely, too, in a media system now so dominated by so few corporations, a consequence of privatization for Australia is that even less cultural and programming diversity will be available than is offered now.

The long-term danger of this scenario is that information will become essentially a privately appropriable commodity; only the wealthy will be able to afford high-cost specialized information and cultural services. Therein lie the beginnings of new class cleavages in Australian society.

## Scenario three: Australia remains with its present mix of public and private institutions in communications, and develops strategies to explore export markets for Australian technological and cultural products

The niche market strategy is one in which Australian firms are given encouragement and support in seeking international markets for high-tech. exports. The strategy is dependent upon the existence of a burgeoning high-tech. infrastructure at home from which successful products can—in theory—make their mark on some world stage. Ideally the domestic market provides the assured base generating the cash flow and profits to fund the export push and foster the development of a local pool of technological expertise. Though, of course, the larger the home market the better the prospect of success, there are some countries which have developed successful export markets from a relatively small domestic base, notably Sweden, Taiwan, Korea and Singapore.

The crux of a niche market strategy is to decide which local products can be best developed, how, and sold to whom. Perceptions vary widely on our best prospects. For instance, the comprehensive Scott Little report, *Information Technology in Australia*, argued that Australia should be 'pursuing the vast potential of the export area'.[11] This report excluded from its top priority list general-purpose computer systems, general-purpose terminals, peripherals and storage devices, personal computers, standard telecommunications devices, standard-memory hard-logic components and consumer electronic products. Moreover, according to the report, 'information services such as cable television, videotex and teletext do not present very attractive market opportunities for local IT suppliers'.[12] Scott Little, who used a broad definition of the term 'information technology', argued that we were most likely to enjoy competitive success in areas such as scientific instruments, software, systems engineering products, and special-purpose applications. For them the important areas of emerging technology with product development opportunities over the next ten to fifteen years included voice recognition and synthesis, flat panel displays, mass (optical) memories, artificial intelligence, parallel processing and image processing.

The Hawke government's technology strategy was closer to this third scenario than any other. Though it achieved more in terms of policy initiatives in science and technology than its predecessors, the Hawke government essentially opted for a cautious status quo approach. Under Labor, Telecom's public monopoly was guaranteed, and Aussat, proposed by the Fraser administration to have a 49 per cent private shareholding, became a commercial company with the Commonwealth government and Telecom as joint public shareholders.

New measures for industry support were initiated—increased grants through the Australian Industrial Research and Development Initiative Scheme, venture capital support through its management and investment companies, tax write-offs of 150 per cent for new product development, and some support for local procurement policies designed to provide access to government markets. These are all commendable, yet essentially moderate initiatives.

What was not embraced by the Hawke administration was the notion of an information society being central to their macro-economic strategy and the need for appropriate social institutions to manage processes of technological change.

## Scenario four: Australia develops coherent national information society policies that will fully develop opportunities in information and communications technologies

Advocates of this direction call for a bold public policy model for economic and social engineering towards an Australian information society. They would argue that if we are to benefit from the growth of information facilities and services in the long run, then we must utilize this trend to redress fundamental structural problems within the Australian economy—contemporary de-industrialization and our status as a technological client state.

Not only do we need a commitment from a national government to tackle structural economic problems but we need to agonize over the planning and institutional mechanisms for economic and social change. What we need is a national strategic planning authority (or authorities) which would encompass a more broadly based EPAC (Economic Planning and Advisory Committee), a high-level Commission for the Future, and possibly the establishment of an Australian Ministry of International Trade and Industry.

The essence of a MITI is targeted industrial concentration, where state-directed planning and finance are provided to secure a dynamic indigenous base. What must be understood about this model is that though the state is the prime architect of strategic economic planning it is the private sector that is supported, stimulated and rewarded for its successful industrial ventures. Critics of the concept argue that a MITI model is high risk for Australia at a time of record government deficits, and that government involvement is antagonistic to the process of commercial innovation.

An Australian MITI would probably identify the communications and information technology field as one for targeted industrial concentration. In the telecommunications area, part of the strategy might be that Telecom, Aussat and OTC would have designated pump-priming roles to stimulate local producers and suppliers. Australia, with its monopolistic public telecommunications authorities, has not followed the European pattern of linking the monopoly position of postal, tele-phone and telegraph services with strong national procurement poli-cies to support indigenous industry. Telecom, for instance, with outlays of more than $1 billion annually on telecommunications equipment, could progressively move towards purchasing from com-panies which were Australian-owned and -controlled. While recent legislation now allows Telecom to establish satellite companies with local engineering firms, Telecom's management has tended to see its role as essentially that of service provider. Under a MITI, a national information policy strategy would call for Telecom to become a bolder local engineering catalyst. As well, policies could be developed to ensure large-scale purchase by public institutions of local computer systems and a national satellite policy (in a country which is now one of the major satellite markets of the world) designed to provide sub-stantial advantages to local manufacturers.

Recent government reports into Australia's telecommunications industry have highlighted inherent key problems, and the major recommendations fit comfortably with the notion of an Australian MITI. A report from the Australian Science and Technology Council (ASTEC) argued that 'a co-ordinated national effort is required to promote development of a more vigorous, export-oriented telecom-munications product development industry'.[13] They call for the establishment of an Australian company to exploit the substantial opportunities in the field of telecommunications product develop-ment and marketing. Shareholders of this company would be the principal government-owned service providers (Telecom, OTC, Aus-sat) and Australian telecommunications equipment manufacturers who wished to co-operate, such as AWA. The company's shareholders would, of course, determine its aims, but the rationale behind its for-mation was to concentrate on the development and marketing, both locally and overseas, of products derived from indigenous R & D. According to ASTEC, the establishment of such a company 'represents the most practical, flexible and market-oriented way to overcome the problems of the Australian telecommunications product industry'.

A subsequent government report, which also called for collabora-tive ventures amongst Australia's public telecommunications autho-rities, was strongly critical of Australia's gross under-investment in new telecommunications networks. This report, by OECD expert Henry Ergas, argued that financial restraints have had a major impact on the efficiency of the Australian telecommunications system.[14] Ergas recommended a substantial reduction in the dividends paid to government, as well as an easing of external borrowing restrictions on OTC and Telecom. The report was critical of the telecommunications industry's low level of spending on R & D and recommended an increase in capital investment of 10–15 per cent in real terms, with an initial rise being followed by 4–8 per cent annual real growth. Ergas argued that an upgrading of the telecommunications network could provide the impetus needed for development of a technologically advanced, research-oriented industry with considerable export potential for Australia.

The acceptance of a MITI model for technological strategic planning requires greater public consciousness of structural economic problems, and a more enlightened approach towards public planning. A MITI model is highly nationalist and requires enormous political will by government and the people to succeed.

What then of these four scenarios? A global revolution is under way and if Australia wants to maintain its standard of living it must seek out its own opportunities in the contemporary technological revolution. Australia must reduce its high dependence on imported technology, strengthen its indigenous product development, and redress its status as a client state for so many overseas interests. Social policies for the information age must be commensurate with measures to ensure long-term economic growth. We urgently need to review how to make decisions about technology in Australian society, and reassess how well our current institutions will serve community needs in the future.

# LIST OF CONTRIBUTORS

Barry Jones, Minister for Science and Small Business.

Professor Don Lamberton, Information Research Unit, Department of Economics, University of Queensland.

Dr Thomas Mandeville, Information Research Unit, Department of Economics, University of Queensland.

Ashley Goldsworthy, Australia's National Information Technology Council.

John Burke, Commission for the Future (formerly executive officer of Victorian Citizens Advice Bureaus).

Marie Keir, Australian Science and Technology Council.

Ian Reinecke, Department of History and Philosophy of Science, Wollongong University.

Averill Edwards, National Library of Australia.

Geoffrey Layzell Ward, Western Australian Department of Computing and Information Technology.

Dr John Langdale, School of Earth Sciences, Macquarie University.

Justice Michael Kirby, New South Wales Court of Appeal.

Trevor Barr, Swinburne Institute of Technology and the Commission for the Future.

# NOTES AND REFERENCES

## 1 TOWARDS A NATIONAL INFORMATION POLICY

1 T. Mandeville and S. Macdonald, 'Technological Change and Employment in the Information Economy: the Example of Queensland', *Prometheus* 3, 1 (1985), pp. 71–85.
2 S. Nora and A. Minc, *The Computerization of Information: a report to the President of France*, Massachusetts Institute of Technology Press, Cambridge, Massachusetts, 1980.

## 2 THE AUSTRALIAN INFORMATION ECONOMY

1 Don Aitkin, 'An R & D Led Recovery', *National Times on Sunday*, 31 August 1986, p. 35. A good corrective to this kind of reasoning is provided by R. R. Nelson, 'Production Sets, Technological Knowledge, and R & D: Fragile and Overworked Constructs for Analysis of Productivity Growth?', *American Economic Review* 70, 2 (1980), pp. 62–7.
2 M. W. Browne, 'The Star Wars Spinoff', *New York Times Magazine*, 24 August 1986, pp. 18–24, 26, 66–7, 69, 73.
3 Harlan Cleveland, 'King Canute and the Information Resource', *Technology Review* 87, 1 (1984), p. 12.
4 J. R. Beniger, *The Control Revolution: Technological and Economic Origins of the Information Society*, Harvard University Press, Cambridge, Massachusetts, 1986.
5 F. H. Knight, *Risk, Uncertainty and Profit*, Houghton Mifflin, New York, 1921, pp. 239, 250, 260–2.
6 D. McQuail, *Communication*, Longman, New York, 1975.
7 E. L. Sommerlad, *National Communication Systems: Some Policy Issues and Options*, UNESCO, Paris, 1975, p. 7.
8 *Economist*, 20 August 1977, p. 91.
9 W. Kunz and H. W. J. Rittel, 'Information Science: On the Structure of its Problems', *Information Storage and Retrieval* 8 (1972), p. 95.
10 F. A. von Hayek, 'Economics and Knowledge', *Economica* 4 (1937), pp. 33–54; 'The Use of Knowledge in Society', *American Economic Review* 35 (1945), pp. 519–30; and 'The Pretence of Knowledge', *Swedish Journal of Economics* 77, 4 (1975), pp. 433–42.

11 D. Starrett, 'Social Institutions, Imperfect Information, and the Distribution of Income', *Quarterly Journal of Economics* 90, 2 (1976), p. 282.

12 W. J. Samuels, 'Information Systems, Preferences, and the Economy in the JEI', *Journal of Economic Issues* 12 (March 1977), p. 25.

13 Cf. T. C. Koopmans and J. M. Montias, 'On the Description and Comparison of Economic Systems' in A. Eckstein (ed.), *Comparison of Economic systems*, University of California Press, Berkeley, p. 57.

14 See D. M. Lamberton, 'Structure and Growth of the Communications Industry', in K. A. Tucker (ed.), *The Economics of the Australian Service Sector*, Croom Helm, London, 1977, p. 145.

15 The standard methods of information-sector accounting have overstated the size of the primary sector because they fail to exclude the 'non-information' component within what are taken to be 'information' activities. See M. R. Rubin and M. T. Huber, *The Knowledge Industry in the United States 1960–1980*, Princeton University Press, Princeton, NJ, 1986, Chapter II.

16 N. Karunaratne, 'A Methodology for the Input-Output Analysis of the Information Economy', quoted by H.-J. Engelbrecht, 'An Exposition of the Information Sector Approach with Special Reference to Australia', *Prometheus* 3, 2 (1985), p. 382.

17 D. M. Lamberton (ed.), *Economics, Information and Knowledge*, Penguin, Harmondsworth, 1971.

18 C. C. von Weizsäcker, 'The Costs of Substitution', *Econometrica* 52, 5 (1984), p. 1085. For a review of this development see D. M. Lamberton, 'The Economics of Information and Organization', in Martha E. Williams (ed.), *Annual Review of Information Science and Technology (ARIST)*, vol. 19, Knowledge Industry Publications for American Society for Information Science, 1984, pp. 3–30.

19 J. E. Stiglitz, 'Information and Economic Analysis: A Perspective', *Economic Journal*, supplement to vol. 95, pp. 21–2.

20 J. Green, 'Differential Information, the Market and Incentive Compatibility', in K. J. Arrow and S. Honkapohja (eds), *Frontiers of Economics*, Blackwell, Oxford, 1985, p. 178.

21 R. E. Hall and J. B. Taylor, *Macroeconomics*, W. W. Norton, New York, 1986, p. 16.

22 K. J. Arrow, *Collected Papers: Vol. 4, The Economics of Information*, Blackwell, Oxford, 1984, p. 138.

23 F. H. Gruen, 'How Bad is Australia's Economic Performance and Why?', *Economic Record* 62, 177 (1986), pp. 180–93.

24 E. F. Denison, *Why Growth Rates Differ: Post War Experience in Nine Western Countries*, Brookings Institution, Washington, DC, 1967.

25 Gruen, op. cit., p. 185.

26 E. F. Denison, 'Explanations of Declining Productivity Growth', *Survey of Current Business* 59, 8 (1979), pp. 1–24.

27 'America the sluggish', *Economist*, 26 July 1980, pp. 14, 17.

28 Weizsäcker, op. cit., p. 1085.

29 For development of this theme see D. M. Lamberton, *Optimal Telecommunications Investment in the Development Process*, International Telecommunications Union, Geneva, 1986.

30 'The Information Business', *Business Week*, 25 August 1986, pp. 82–6, 90.

31 P. W. Strassman, *Information Payoff: The Transformation of Work in the Electronic Age*, Free Press, New York, 1985.

32 D. M. Lamberton, S. Macdonald and T. D. Mandeville, 'Productivity and

Technological Change: Towards an Alternative to Myers' Hypothesis', *Canberra Bulletin of Public Administration* IX, 2 (1982), pp. 23–30.

[33] T. Mandeville, S. Macdonald, B. Thompson and D. M. Lamberton, *Technology, Employment and the Queensland Information Economy*, University of Queensland Information Research Unit, Brisbane, 1984; D. M. Lamberton and B. Thompson, *New Office Technology*, Australian Government Publishing Service, Canberra, 1985.

[34] op. cit., p. 186. See Mancur Olson, *The Rise and Decline of Nations: Economic Growth, Stagflation and Social Rigidities*, Yale University Press, New Haven, 1982.

[35] J. A. Schumpeter, *Capitalism, Socialism, and Democracy*, Harper and Row, New York, 1942; C. P. Kindleberger, 'The Aging Economy', *Weltwirtschaftliches Archiv* 114, 3 (1978), pp. 407–21.

[36] R. D. Norton, 'Industrial Policy and American Renewal', *Journal of Economic Literature* 24, 1 (1986), p. 20.

[37] Gruen, op. cit., p. 193.

[38] T. Barr, *The Electronic Estate*, Penguin, Melbourne, 1985, p. 13.

[39] S. S. Roach, 'Macrorealities of the Information Economy', in R. Landau and N. Rosenberg (eds), *The Positive Sum Strategy: Harnessing Technology for Economic Growth*, National Academy Press, Washington, DC, 1986, pp. 93–103.

[40] ibid., p. 97.

[41] The measures of capital are of the conventional kind and fail to include information and information channels.

[42] Roach, op. cit., pp. 101–2.

[43] Helen Meredith, 'Computers—Your Stake in the Future', *Australian*, 7 October 1986, p. 7. The effect of recent price changes should be noted, e.g., IBM's decision to lift prices by 15 per cent—see *Australian*, 7 October 1986, p. 19.

[44] Bill Caelli, 'Import Bill Points to R & D Failings', *Australian*, 27 May 1986, p. 30.

[45] Meredith, op. cit., p. 9.

[46] Ashley Goldsworthy, *Courier-Mail*, 3 June 1986, p. 26.

[47] Australian Science and Technology Council [ASTEC], 'Table C-3. Indices of Revealed, Comparative Advantage in Invention, 1970–79', *Telecommunications Research and Development in Australia*, Australian Government Publishing Service, Canberra, 1985.

[48] See, for example, R. G. Gregory, 'Industry Protection and Adjustment: The Australian Experience', *Prometheus* 3, 1 (1985), p. 26.

[49] See Department of Science, 'A National Information Policy for Australia', discussion paper, Department of Science, Canberra, 1985.

[50] See, for example, M. Jussawalla, N. D. Karunaratne and D. M. Lamberton (eds), *The Cost of Thinking: The Primary Information Sector of 10 Pacific Basin Countries*, Ablex Publishing, New Jersey, forthcoming.

[51] As reported in National Institute for Research Advancement, *Comprehensive Study of Microelectronics 1985*, NIRA, Tokyo, 1985, p. 98.

[52] 'Nobel Winner Engrossed by Balancing Act', *New York Times*, 26 November 1972, p. F5.

## 3 AN INTERNATIONAL COMPARISON

[1] F. Machlup, *The Production and Distribution of Knowledge in the United States*, Princeton University Press, Princeton, NJ, 1962.

2 D. Bell, *The Coming of Post-Industrial Society*, Basic Books, New York, 1973.
3 M. U. Porat, *The Information Economy: Definition and Measurement*, nine volumes, US Government Printing Office, Washington, DC, 1977.
4 OECD, *Information Activities, Electronics and Telecommunications Technologists*, Paris, 1981.
5 D. M. Lamberton, 'Australia as an Information Society—Who Calls the Shots?', in Department of Science and Technology, *National Technology Conference*, Australian Government Publishing Service, Canberra, 1984, pp. 125–31.
6 E.g., N. Karunaratne, The Information Age and the Larger ASEAN Economies, and Pacific Islands and the Information Age, papers presented to the workshop on measurement of the primary information sectors of ten Pacific region countries, East-West Centre, University of Hawaii, 1984; H.-J. Engelbrecht, From Newly Industrialising to Newly Informatising Country: the Primary Information Sector of the Republic of Korea, 1975–1980, paper presented to the 14th conference of economists, University of NSW, Sydney, May 1985.
7 R. Yin-Wang Kwok and B. Kit-Ying Au, 'The Information Industry, Multinational Corporations and Urbanisation in the Asian Pacific Countries: A Research Agenda', *Prometheus* 3, 2 (1985), pp. 349–69.
8 H. Bergendorff, 'International Data Communications in the OECD Area: 1976 and 1981', OECD, Paris, 1982, DSTI/ICCP/82.27.
9 D. M. Lamberton, 'Structure and Growth of the Communications Industry', in K. A. Tucker (ed.), *The Economics of the Australian Service Sector*, Croom Helm, London, 1977, pp. 143–66. See also Javes' work, reported in Barry Jones, *Sleepers, Wake! Technology and the Future of Work*, Oxford University Press, Melbourne, 1982, Chapter 3.
10 OECD, 'Updating of the Data Base Combined in OECD–ICCP publication no. 6, vol. 1', Paris, February 1984.
11 T. Mandeville, S. Macdonald, B. Thompson, and D. M. Lamberton, *Technology, Employment and the Queensland Information Economy*, Information Research Unit, Department of Economics, University of Queensland, October 1983. A summary of that study is contained in T. Mandeville and S. Macdonald, 'Technological Change and Employment in the Information Economy: the Example of Queensland', *Prometheus* 3, 1 (1985), pp. 71–85.
12 Bergendorff, op. cit.
13 D. M. Lamberton and T. D. Mandeville, 'Transborder Data Flows and large Australian Companies', report to OECD and Australian Department of Communications, March 1983.
14 E. Nerberger, 'Libermanism, Computopia and Visible Hand: The Question of Informational Efficiency', *American Economic Review* 56, 2 (1966), pp. 131–44.
15 Department of Science, 'A National Information Policy for Australia', discussion paper, Department of Science, Canberra, 1985.

## 4 EXPANDING ECONOMIC HORIZONS

1 D. M. Lamberton, 'Information Age Economics', in *Technological Change— Impact of Information Technology 1984*, Canberra Publishing and Printing Co., pp. 3–13.
2 *Australian*, 26 April 1986, p. 15.
3 E. R. Cawthron and J. Felsinger, *Optical Communications and Fibre Optics: Australian Capabilities and Opportunities*, Department of Industry, Technology and Commerce, 1986.

⁴ T. Luckyj, *Expert Systems: Australian Capabilities and Opportunities*, Department of Industry, Technology and Commerce, 1986.

⁵ Luckyj, op, cit., p. 21.

⁶ W. D. Scott & Co. Pty Ltd in association with Arthur D. Little Inc., *Information Technology in Australia, Capabilities and Opportunities*, 2 vols, Department of Science and Technology, 1984.

⁷ Committee of Inquiry into Education and Training (chairman Bruce Williams), *Education, Training and Employment*, Australian Government Publishing Service, Canberra, 1979.

⁸ *Information Technology in Australia*, op. cit.

## 5  THE IMPACT OF TECHNOLOGY ON COMMUNITY INFORMATION PROCESSES

¹ National Consumer Council, *The Fourth Right of Citizenship, A review of local advice services*, National Consumer Council, London, 1977.

² Department of Science, *Discussion Paper: A National Information Policy for Australia*, Canberra Publishing and Printing Co., Canberra, 1985, p. 37.

³ See, for example, Department of Prime Minister and Cabinet, *Task Force on Government Information: Report*, Australian Government Publishing Service, Canberra, 1980, Chapter 5.

⁴ C. Williamson, Information seeking by users of a Citizens' Advice Bureau, Master of Librarianship thesis, Monash University, 1984, p. 95.

⁵ J. Burke, 'Computer Technology and Citizens Advice Bureaus', *Information Interchange* 5, 1 (1985), pp. 3–12.

⁶ The policy document arising from this conference is available from the Commission for the Future, Melbourne.

⁷ Priorities Review Staff, *Goals and Strategies*, Australian Government Publishing Service, Canberra, 1973, p. 35.

⁸ J. Weizenbaum, *Science*, 12 May 1972, pp. 609–14.

⁹ This need has led to the development of a community interest computer consultancy project in Victoria, under the auspices of the Victorian Council of Social Service and the Royal Melbourne Institute of Technology.

## 6  BRAVE NEW WIRED WORLD

¹ Adapted from D. Van Tassel, 'Daily Surveillance Sheet 1987 From a Nationwide Data Bank', *Computers and People* 24, 31 August 1985.

² *Australian Financial Review*, 18 July 1986, p. 3.

³ The discussion of EFTPOS is based on an Australian Science and Technology Council (ASTEC) report to the Prime Minister, *Towards a Cashless Society?*, Australian Government Publishing Service, Canberra, 1986. Detailed references for the discussion can be found in that report.

⁴ *Comprehensive Study of Microelectronics 1985*, National Institute for Research Advancement, Tokyo.

⁵ Roland Tellzen, 'Automated tellers boost service scope', *Australian*, 29 July 1986.

⁶ Rex Malik, 'Beyond the exponential cascade', *Journal of the International Institute of Communications*, reprinted as 'The Goddam Turnpike Theory—international computer banking goes out of control', *Australian*, 3 June 1986, pp. 34, 35, 50.

⁷ *Towards a Cashless Society?*, op. cit.

8 Harry Kalven Jr, 'The problems of privacy in the year 2000', *Daedalus*, summer 1967, pp. 876–82.
9 Sherry Turkle, *The Second Self: Computers and the Human Spirit*, Granada, New York, 1984, p. 51.
10 Pamela McCorduck, *Machines Who Think*, W. H. Freeman, San Francisco, 1979, pp. 253–5.
11 Advertisement in *Aviation Week and Space Technology*, 17 February 1986, p. 121.
12 For a longer discussion see *Network New Zealand: Communications in the Future*, Commission for the Future, Wellington, 1981.
13 *Towards a Cashless Society?*, p. 100.
14 These questions are discussed in *Towards a Cashless Society?*, pp. 157–8.
15 Lynn White, *Medieval Technology and Social Change*, Oxford University Press, New York, 1966, p. 28.

# 7 WEALTH AND POVERTY IN THE INFORMATION SOCIETY

1 B. Jones, *Sleepers, Wake! Technology and the Future of Work*, Oxford University Press, Melbourne, 1982, p. 173.
2 J. Kozol, *Illiterate America*, Anchor Press/Doubleday, New York, 1985, p. 4.
3 For a fuller account of the micro-computer boom, the factors that fuelled and deflated it, see I. Reinecke, *Micro Computers*, Penguin, Melbourne, 1983.
4 The French experience is covered in more detail in I. Reinecke, *Connecting You . . .*, McPhee Gribble/Penguin, Melbourne, 1985, pp. 78–82.
5 One of the more fanciful of such accounts is by John Madden, 'Julia's Dilemma', in D. Godfrey and D. Parkhill, *Gutenberg Two*, Press Porcepic, Toronto, 1980, pp. 13ff.
6 W. Dizard, *The Coming Information Age*, Longman, New York, 1982, p. 11.
7 D. Bell, *The Coming of Post-Industrial Society*, Basic Books, New York, 1976, p. 228.
8 ibid, pp. 27–33.
9 D. Bell, 'The Year 2000—the Trajectory of an Idea', in Daniel Bell (ed.), *Toward the Year 2000: Work in Progress*, Beacon Press, Boston, 1969, p. 4.
10 J. K. Galbraith, *The New Industrial State*, Houghton Mifflin, Boston, 1979, p. 176.
11 L. Winner, *Autonomous Technology*, Massachusetts Institute of Technology Press, Cambridge, Massachusetts, 1977, p. 164.
12 A. Toffler, *Previews and Premises*, William Morrow, New York, 1983, p. 112.
13 Jones, op. cit., p. 188.
14 ibid., p. 184.
15 See I. Reinecke and J. Schultz, *The Phone Book*, Penguin, Melbourne, 1983 and Reinecke, *Connecting You . . .*, op. cit.
16 Patricia Glass Schuman, *Library and Information Service for Meeting Personal Needs*, White House conference on Library and Information Services, Washington, DC, October 1979, pp. 9, 18.
17 For more detail about this project and another similar one, see Reinecke, *Connecting You . . .*, op. cit., pp. 175–89.

## 8 LIBRARY RESOURCES IN THE AGE OF INFORMATION TECHNOLOGY

1. S. Wannen, 'The Bulletin goes online for easy reference', *Bulletin* 108, 5527 (July 1986), p. 44.

2. A. Oxley, 'Managing the information manager', *The Information Professional*, proceedings of a conference November 1984, Riverina-Murray Institute for Higher Education, Wagga Wagga, 1985, pp. 7–16.

3. A. B. Veanor, '1985–1995: the next decade in academic librarianship Part I', *College and Research Libraries* 46, 3 (1985), pp. 209–29.

4. I. McCallum, 'Libraries, life quality and appropriate technology—lessons or lesions', *Lifestyles and Libraries: proceedings of the Library Association of Australia Conference, 1986*, Library Association of Australia, Sydney, 1986.

5. Ching-Chih, Chen, 'Interactive videodisc technology and the future of information provision', *Lifestyles and Libraries*, op. cit.

6. E. Wainwright, 'The university, its library and the information age', *Australian Academic and Research Libraries* 6, 2 (1985), pp. 65–80.

7. National Library of Australia *'Twenty-Fifth Annual Report 1984–85'*, National Library of Australia, Canberra, 1985, p. 57.

8. 'Library statistics 1984', *Australian Academic and Research Libraries*, Supplement 16, 3 (1985), p. xii.

9. A. B. Veanor, '1985–1995: the next decade in academic librarianship Part II', *College and Research Libraries* 46, 4 (1985), p. 301.

10. W. Horton, A. Hazell, J. Adams, *'Report of the Corporate Plan and Review Committee'*, Library Association of Australia, Sydney, 1986, Appendix 1.

11. ibid., p. 17.

12. For example, UNESCO, Department of International Economic and Social Affairs, Statistical Office, *'1982 Statistical Yearbook'*, United Nations, Paris, 1985, p. 435.

13. W. Horton, 'The National Library of Australia: future directions', *Lifestyles and Libraries*, op. cit., p. 23.

14. M. Gorman, 'Laying siege to the "fortress library"', *American Libraries* 17, 5 (1986), pp. 325–8.

15. P. Battin, Edited testimony given to the United States House of Representatives Committee on Science and Technology Task Force on Science Policy Hearing, *Information Hotline* 18, 6 (1986), pp. 15–18.

16. Library Association of Australia, 'Statement on Free Library Service to All', *Handbook*, LAA, Sydney, 1984, p. 82.

17. I.Reinecke, 'Information justice', *Lifestyles and Libraries*, op. cit.

18. Australia, Parliament, Senate, *Daily Hansard*, 11 June 1986, pp. 3727–36.

19. Library Association of Australia, 'Draft statement on National Information Policy in the LAA', General Council papers, November 1985, LAA, Sydney, 1985, pp. 82–90.

20. Australian Libraries and Information Council, *Annual Report for the period to 30 June 1983*, ALIC, Canberra, 1983, p. 6.

21. Australian Libraries and Information Council, *Plan for library and related information services in Australia*, ALIC, Canberra, 1983, p. 4.

22. Department of Science, 'A National Information Policy for Australia', discussion paper, Department of Science, Canberra, 1985.

23. Department of Science, *National Information Policy Workshop*, Department of Science, Canberra, 1986, p. 56.

[24] Department of Science, 'Scientific and Technological Information: proceedings of a workshop, Canberra, 20 March 1986', Department of Science, Canberra, 1986, p. 43.

[25] D. I. Raitt, 'Look no paper/the library of tomorrow', *Electronic Library* 3, 4 (1985), pp. 276–89.

[26] Wainwright, op. cit., p. 78.

[27] T. T. Surprenant and C. Perry-Holmes, 'The reference librarian of the future: a scenario', *Reference Quarterly* 25, 2 (1985), pp. 234–8.

[28] op. cit., p. 236.

[29] Veanor, Part I, op. cit.

## 10 INFORMATION TECHNOLOGY POLICY IN WESTERN AUSTRALIA

[1] *Information technology study: community perceptions: implications for Western Australian policy development*, Western Australian Science, Industry, and Technology Council, Perth, 1986.

[2] Western Australian Legislative Assembly, *Hansard*, 1983, pp. 5091ff.

[3] ibid., 1984, pp. 4147ff.

[4] B. Jones, *Sleepers, Wake! Technology and the Future of Work*, Oxford University Press, Melbourne, 1982.

## 11 TRANSBORDER DATA FLOWS AND NATIONAL SOVEREIGNTY

[1] On Third World countries, see C. J. Hamelink, *Cultural Autonomy in Global Communications*, Longman, New York, 1983, pp. 91–4. On France, see S. Nora and A. Minc, *The Computerization of Society*, Massachusetts Institute of Technology Press, Cambridge, Massachusetts, and A. Madec, 'The Political Economy of Information Flows', *Inter Media* 9, 2 (1980), pp. 29–32. On Canada, see Consultative Committee on the Implications of Telecommunications for Canadian Sovereignty, *Telecommunications and Canada*, (the Clyne Report), Ottawa, 1979. On Sweden, see U. Tengelin, 'A Computer Society is too Vulnerable', *Inter Media* 9, 2 (1981), pp. 33–5. On Australia, see Department of Science, 'A National Information Policy for Australia', discussion paper, Department of Science, Canberra, 1985, and J. V. Langdale, *Transborder Data Flow and International Trade in Electronic Information Services: an Australian Perspective* (a Report to the Department of Communications), Australian Government Publishing Service, Canberra, 1985.

[2] *Long-Range Goals in International Telecommunications and Information: An Outline for United States Policy*, Report to the Congress of the United States by the National Telecommunications and Information Administration, Washington, DC, 1983.

[3] Australian Telecommunications Commission, *Annual Report*, Melbourne, 1980 and 1985.

[4] Overseas Telecommunications Commission, *Annual Report*, Sydney, 1980 and 1985.

[5] B. Robins, 'OTC Announces $2 bn Modernisation Plan', *Australian Financial Review*, 27 June 1986, p. 33.

[6] United Nations Centre on Transnational Corporations, *Transnational Corporations and Transborder Data Flows*, United Nations, New York, 1982, pp. 59–61.

7   P. Robinson, 'Sovereignty and Data: Some Perspectives', *Transnational Data Report 7*, 7 (1984), pp. 419–21.

8   H. Mowlana, *International Flow of Information: A Global Report and Analysis*, Reports and Papers on Mass Communications, No. 99, UNESCO, Paris, 1985.

9   J. V. Langdale, 'International Competition: Communication Services', *Media Information Australia* 38, November 1985, pp. 112–15.

10  Australia. Joint Committee on Foreign Affairs and Defence, *Australian-United States' Relations: The Extraterritorial Application of United States Laws*, Australian Government Publishing Service, Canberra, 1983.

11. J. R. S. Revell, *Banking and Electronic Funds Transfer*, OECD, Paris, 1983.

## 12  NEW TECHNOLOGY AND INTERNATIONAL PRIVACY ISSUES

1   Garry Marx, 'I'll Be Watching You', *Dissent*, Winter 1985.

2   T. Riley, 'Privacy in the 1980s—Another Trade Barrier?', *Journal of Commerce*, 17 October 1985, p. 1.

3   L. J. Curtis, Administrative Law Reform—Impact on Public Sector Management, unpublished paper for the National Government Accounting Convention, University of Adelaide, 21 February 1985.

4   *Freedom of Information Act*, 5 USC 552 (United States); *Access to Information Act* 1983 (Canada); *Privacy Act* 1983 (Canada).

5   P. Kellner, 'All so Wrong about Rights', *The Times*, 1 July 1985.

6   Reported in the *Economist*, 16 February 1985.

7   *Official Information Act* 1982 (New Zealand).

8   Cf. I. Eagles and M. Taggart, Report on Reform of Official Information Act 1982, prepared at the direction of the Hon. G. W. R. Palmer, Minister of Justice and Attorney-General, mimeo, October 1984.

9   *Freedom of Information Act* 1982 (Aust.) ss.11, 48. See G. J. Evans (1984), 9 *Commonwealth Record* 2537.

10  Australia. Department of Health, *Towards Fairness and Equity: The Australia Card Program*, Department of Health, Canberra, 1986.

11  T. Riley (ed.), *Access to Government Documents: Some International Perspectives and Trends*, forthcoming.

12  Australia. Attorney-General's Department, Freedom of Information Act 1982, *Annual Report 1983–84*, Australian Government Publishing Service, Canberra, 1985, pp. 107–9.

13  Human Experimentation Bill 1985 (Aust.).

14  *Osmond v. Public Service Board of New South Wales* [1984] 3 NSWLR 447; [1985] LRC (Const.) 1041.

15  *Public Service Board of New South Wales v. Osmond*, unreported, High Court of Australia, 21 February 1986.

16  J. Bing, P. Forsberg and E. Nygaard, Legal Problems related to transborder data Flows: an exploration, unpublished paper prepared for OECD, Paris, 1983, pp. 59ff.

17  N. Blewett, Minister for Health, news release, Canberra, 10 February 1986.

18  M. Bouchard, Administrative Law in the Real World: A Canadian Perspective, unpublished paper to New Zealand Legal Research Foundation seminar on judicial review of administrative action, Auckland, February 1986.

19  See, for example, Senator P. Walsh, Minister for Finance, in Australia, Senate, *Debates*, 17 April 1985.

[20] J. Howard (opposition leader) in an address given shortly after his election as leader of the opposition.

## 13 WHOSE REVOLUTION?

[1] See T. Barr, *The Electronic Estate: New Communications Media and Australia*, Penguin, Melbourne, 1985.
[2] W. D. Scott & Co. Pty Ltd in association with Arthur D. Little Inc., *Information Technology in Australia: Capabilities and Opportunities*, Department of Science and Technology, Canberra, 1984, vol. 1, p. 13.
[3] See Chapter 4.
[4] These arguments have already been developed by Averill Edwards in Chapter 8.
[5] *Nature* 316, 18 July 1985, pp. 185–6.
[6] M. Pirie, 'Everyone Benefits from Privatisation', *Institute of Public Affairs Review* 39, 3 (1985–86).
[7] Business Telecommunications Services Pty Ltd, Submission to the Public Inquiry into Telecommunications Services in Australia, December 1981.
[8] C. D. Trengove, *Telecommunications in Australia: Competition or Monopoly?*, Centre of Policy Studies, Monash University, 1982.
[9] See Chapter 6 of Barr, *The Electronic Estate*, op. cit.
[10] ibid., pp. 217–21.
[11] W. D. Scott & Co. Pty Ltd in association with Arthur D. Little Inc., *Information Technology in Australia: Capabilities and Opportunities*, Department of Science and Technology, Canberra, 1984, vol. 1, p. 24.
[12] ibid., vol. 2, p. A–43.
[13] Australian Science and Technology Council, *Telecommunications Research and Development in Australia*, Australian Government Publishing Service, Canberra, 1985.
[14] H. Ergas, *Telecommunications and the Australian Economy*, Department of Communications, Australian Government Publishing Service, Canberra, 1986.

# INDEX